W9-AEZ-063

ANCIENT CHINA

Ancient China

FROM THE BEGINNINGS TO THE EMPIRE

Jacques Gernet

TRANSLATED FROM THE FRENCH BY

Raymond Rudorff

UNIVERSITY OF CALIFORNIA PRESS
Berkeley and Los Angeles: 1968

University of California Press
Berkeley and Los Angeles, California

Library of Congress Catalog Card Number 68–19988

Originally published by
Presses Universitaires de France
as
'La Chine Ancienne'

Printed in Great Britain

CONTENTS

CONTENTS

MAPS

INTRODUCTION

INTRODUCTION

This history covers a period of fifteen hundred years, from the beginnings of Chinese civilization to the foundation of the Empire in 221 B.C.

A thousand years may count for little in the history of China. But it is worth bearing in mind what an astonishing evolution it underwent from the Neolithic period to the time it became a vast centralized empire comparable to the Roman Empire but far more densely populated and very much more advanced technically. Although China is so far away from us, its history is none the less rich and complex. The mass of specialized studies, the number of archaeological discoveries made in China since 1950, and the paucity of comprehensive works covering the period from its earliest beginnings and giving the most recent excavations the recognition they deserve, all make the popular historian's task more difficult. Although he must restrict himself to the most salient developments, he should also ask himself which factors might help to explain and indicate the great dividing dates in Chinese history; thus, where he should only have to give precise details he is often obliged to offer his own personal interpretation.

Admittedly a guiding thread does run through Chinese history, for the whole evolution from the Neolithic cultures established in Northern China in the early second millennium B.C. to the centralized Empire of the Ch'in and Han took place against the background of a gradual modification of the relations between settlers and natural environment. Such factors as the gradual domestication of wild animals, destruction of certain species, selection of plants, and especially progress in land-clearance and cultivation are most enlightening for they all touch essentials. There were several stages here: first of all, a very slow conquest of nature by mankind from the Neolithic to the end of the Bronze Age period, and then, a rapid and complete transformation of the Chinese landscape between the northern steppes and the Yangtse basin with the diffusion of the iron-casting technique from about 500 B.C. onwards. It was then, and only then, that China became the great agricultural empire it was to remain until modern times. Two great technical accomplishments should be remembered, for they brought about profound changes: bronze-casting, which seems to lie at the origin of Chinese civilization, and iron-casting, which made it possible to farm all the plains and rapidly enriched the Chinese world. We need hardly mention that society and political forms changed at the same time as natural conditions, population density, products and techniques. None the less, we think it is necessary to stress this point.

Besides the important technical innovations that brought about social changes (polished stone, bronze-casting, chariots, cast iron and infantry), there are other factors, of a permanent nature, that may help to clarify our ideas; they concern geography and mankind. Such factors present enough contradictions and contrasts to put us on our guard against any simplifications.

To western eyes, China seems to have lived in a kind of isolation. Indeed, in northern China the flat, marshy coasts and the absence of islands made the ancient Chinese turn away from the sea; the mountainous and unhealthy south was only slowly colonized at a comparatively late date; almost impassable mountain chains barred the horizon of the Chinese to the west and south-west, and lastly, the steppes and deserts of Mongolia and Sinkiang (Chinese Turkestan) formed a barrier through which influences from the evolved civilizations of western Asia permeated with difficulty. But, as the whole of Chinese history confirms, this isolation was always relative. In the first place, we could not explain the birth of Chinese civilization, the discovery of metal alloys and the chariot, and the foundation of the first palace-cities in middle Yellow River China if we did not consider far-off influences which may have come from regions to the south of the Ural mountains before they were passed on to the Chinese by the peoples of the steppes. China owes an immense debt to the nomads and the sedentary civilizations of central Asia and the Middle East. Huns, Turks, Mongols, Manchus, Sogdians, Iranians, Indians and Arabs sometimes played a decisive part in Chinese history and also deeply influenced the arts, the techniques, the games, the thought and the religion of the Chinese. Taken as a whole, Chinese history cannot be isolated from that of the other civilizations of Asia. The relations between them were perhaps intermittent, but they were never definitely severed.

From another point of view, given the diversity of geographical and living conditions from Siberia to the extreme south of China, and from the high Tibetan plateaus to the Yangtse delta, we may say that China and its bordering regions alone make up a world as diverse and as full of contrasts as that in which the civilizations of the Near East and the Mediterranean developed.

We should first note that there was a fundamental contrast

between regions suitable for agriculture, where the land had been cleared from Neolithic times onwards (the great alluvial plains of north China and loess plateaus of Shensi and Shansi—loess being a fine sand and clay dust formed by action of the wind), and the northern steppes which were only suitable for pastoral or semi-pastoral ways of life. The relations between the farming peoples of China and the nomadic stock-breeders of the steppes became one of the most important factors in Chinese political and cultural history.

There was also a contrast between the Chinese as possessors of evolved techniques for the organization of open spaces and the very varied primitive peoples who occupied most of the lands which Chinese civilization took over: these peoples were plant-gatherers, hunters, shepherds, itinerant farmers, and the fishermen of the lower Yangtse and Chekiang. From earliest times and during the whole of Chinese history, they were either being slowly assimilated by the Chinese—each mutually influencing the other—or else pushed back into the mountains. Some of them still survive today in the mountainous regions of southern China and in the Indo-Chinese peninsula.

As soon as the regions of the middle and lower Yangtse, which had been barbarian but were slowly colonized from the early first millennium B.C. onwards, began to play a part in history, great differences arose between the way of life, the temperament and the traditions of the North Chinese who were land-owners and corn- and millet-eaters, and the South Chinese who were boatmen, sailors and rice-eaters.

But this general contrast between Yangtse China and Yellow River China covers a diversity of local cultures due to the existence of distinct natural regions. Far from forming a uniform whole, China was composed of a variety of different countries, each with their own history and often with distinct peoples. Each one was more or less isolated by mountain chains, which usually ran from east to west, thus explaining the importance of mountain passes both from a strategic and a commercial point of view (passes between Shensi and Honan, Shansi-Hopei, Shensi-Szechuan and Honan-Hopei). Whereas remote influences were relatively weak and intermittent in China, local influences were always very marked, such as those of indigenous populations and near neighbours (Tibetan shepherds in Szechuan, steppe nomads of Shansi, fishing peoples of the lower Yangtse, etc.). Some of these countries appear very early in Chinese history and sometimes they still correspond to modern provinces. It is necessary to consider the following as fairly distinct regions:

The great northern plain covering the modern provinces of Honan and Hopei, west Shantung and northern Anhwei as far as the Huai valley. It was there that the Bronze Age civilization was born and that the first palace-cities were built;
the Shansi plateau (Chin state);
the Shensi basin, and, in its extension, the Kansu corridor (centre of the Western Chou at the beginning of the first millennium, and later, the Ch'in state);
the Shantung peninsula (Ch'i state);
the basin of the middle Yangtse (Ch'u state);
the plains of the lower Yangtse (southern Kiangsu: Wu state and northern Chekiang: Yueh state);
the red basin of Szechuan (Shu state).

To be complete, this list should also include the maritime and mountain regions of the south-east and the plains near

Canton, but they assumed historical importance at a fairly late date.

Lastly, because China looks so small on maps we are all too liable to forget that it is a country of great distances and areas. The northern plain alone covers an area equal to three quarters of that of France and the remotest capitals of kingdoms in the seventh century B.C. were as far from one another as Rome from Paris. It was only natural that such great distances should have favoured cultural differences and autonomist tendencies.

Complexity, diversity and immensity—these are some of the fundamental characteristics of the Chinese world. If we have dwelt on them it is because they are the points the western reader tends to overlook (1).

SOURCES AND THE CHRONOLOGICAL FRAMEWORK

I

SOURCES AND THE CHRONOLOGICAL FRAMEWORK

1 The Sources

For a long time our knowledge of archaic China was based solely on Chinese literary tradition. Consequently, the picture of ancient China transmitted to Europe by Jesuit missionaries in the eighteenth century was composed of legendary elements, rationalized and woven into a continuous, moralistic history, which dated the beginnings of Chinese civilization back to the early third millennium B.C.

As soon as this orthodox literary tradition became more complex, i.e. from the fifth century B.C. onwards, the behaviour and mentality of archaic China were no longer understood. Vaguely recollected social customs and magical and religious practices were all interpreted as historical events and individual actions, edifying or harmful, that were attributed to the various rulers. But it was only too obvious that the Chinese tradition relating to the remote past was largely without value—on the historical level it claimed for itself—and it was condemned from the Manchu period onwards by free-minded, courageous scholars. On the other hand, archaic themes and fragments of legend which have escaped the theorizing of Chinese historians conceal another form of truth for, although they are difficult to date and to place, a scholar sensitive to social factors may make use of them in an attempt to discover the customs and ideas of a vanished world. Marcel Granet was alone in showing the way and he did so in a masterly fashion, rightly condemning the futility of all attempts at historical reconstruction whilst archaeological evidence was still so scarce and incomplete.

The truth is that excavations only began fairly recently in China. Before the Second World War little was known—and much of that was incorrect—about the prehistory of eastern Asia and it was only in 1928 that the first scientific excavations were carried out in north-eastern Honan on the site of Anyang, which is so important to our knowledge of Shang civilization. Work there was interrupted by the Japanese invasion in 1937. From 1899, when the site was accidentally discovered, until 1928, secret excavations were carried out at Anyang and numerous fakes, which threw discredit on this exceptional discovery, were put on the market by antique dealers as soon as scholars and collectors showed interest in the specimens of archaic writing and bronzes that came from this ancient metropolis.

But thanks to the excavations undertaken at Anyang between 1928 and 1937, and reopened since China became a People's Republic, we now have a very rich body of archaeological evidence to document the state of Chinese civilization between the fourteenth and eleventh centuries B.C. (very numerous inscriptions of undoubted authenticity, ground-plans of palaces, furnaces and foundries, ramparts, great royal tombs, weapons and ritual vases, pottery, chariots, etc.), and the scientific bibliography of the site at Anyang is already extensive. But quite apart from this site, as a result of the major excavations undertaken all over China since 1950, archaeological finds are multiplying at such a rate that work on them fails to keep pace. Bronze Age sites of an earlier date than Anyang have been excavated in

Honan (1) and numerous discoveries have already enabled us to know more about the periods between the end of the Shang period and the foundation of the Empire. Among important discoveries we may mention that of the iron foundries of the Yen kingdom, near Peking, the lacquer work of the Ch'u kingdom from Changsha in Hunan, and the series of intact chariots recently found in Honan. Palaeolithic and Neolithic sites—very rare before the last war—are now counted by the hundred. Over 3,000 sites of the Polished Stone culture have already been located. Many astonishing treasures probably still lie hidden in the soil of China and we have reason to believe that our knowledge of Chinese antiquity and the circumstances in which the Bronze Age civilization arose in the Yellow River basin will be far more precise some ten years hence, when all the newly found archaeological evidence has been exploited.

In spite of the interest and authenticity of the archaeological discoveries that have been made, the fact remains that the actual pattern of Chinese history and, above all, most of what we know of the last five centuries of pre-imperial China derives from relatively abundant written sources. Some of these served as a basis for traditional teaching in imperial China until the beginning of the twentieth century. They are the classics of the Confucian school. Careful philological examination has shown that they contain a number of apocryphal passages written in the Han period or later; and, quite apart from the classics, many other ancient works have been found to be spurious and to have been written at later dates than traditionally supposed. However, these texts are still substantial enough to form part of a history of pre-imperial China, and it is not infrequent for texts and archaeological data to give each other mutual support.

Thanks to the excavations, the comparatively recent idea that the ancient Chinese world underwent an evolution comparable to that of the ancient civilizations of the Near East and the Mediterranean is now beginning to take shape. One of the aims of this short book is to give more substance to the idea.

2 The Chronological Framework

As far as the chronological framework is concerned, we shall distinguish between the following periods:

(*i*) *The Neolithic Period* (from the fourth millennium (?) to the beginning of the second millennium B.C.). Stratigraphy has revealed a succession of Neolithic cultures, mainly in Honan and southern Hopei, the region where the Bronze civilization originated. Some of the Neolithic cultures that evolved at the end of this period may correspond to the more or less legendary Hsia dynasty (traditional dates: twenty-second to nineteenth century B.C.) but Chinese civilization really begins only with the appearance of bronze.

(*ii*) *The Bronze Age* (from the eighteenth century (?) to the end of the sixth century B.C.). The Shang (or Yin) dynasty belongs to this era. Two periods may be distinguished for the Shang: first, the period preceding the establishment of the capital near modern Anyang; second, the final period at Anyang (from the fourteenth to the early eleventh century B.C.; traditional dates: 1384-1111 B.C.). The Chou who succeeded them first settled in the Wei valley in Shensi (whence their name of Western Chou) until the middle of the eighth century. During the following period (seventh and sixth centuries), which corresponds to the beginning of the Eastern Chou (capital at Loyang in north-west Honan), large provincial groupings were formed, and these powerful peripheral kingdoms imposed their rule on the small cities of the great plain. This was the so-called period of the Hegemons, transitional between the archaic period and the forming of states. This period roughly corresponds to that covered by the chronicle of the kingdom of Lu (the *Ch'un-ch'iu* or 'Spring and autumn').

(*iii*) *The beginnings of the Iron Age* (*c.* 500 B.C. until imperial unification in 221 B.C.). Profound changes took place during these three centuries which witnessed the forming of military states (from the middle of the fifth century this period was traditionally known as the epoch of the Warring States). The state structures that arose in the great kingdoms of this period were linked to social and economic changes which were to make China very different from what it had been in the archaic period. The States—especially the Ch'in state in Shensi—were forerunners of the Empire.

Chronological Table

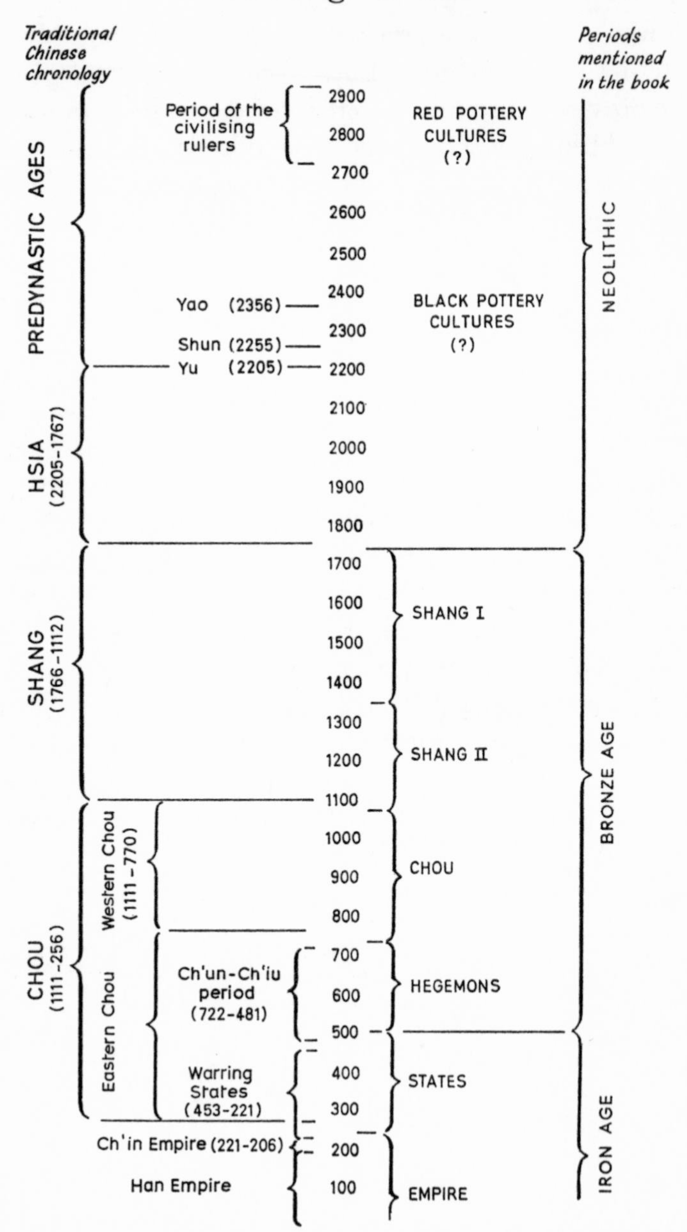

The diffusion of bronze casting techniques, and especially the transition from polished stone to bronze, did not occur as suddenly as the table might suggest.

PREHISTORY AND THE ORIGINS OF CHINESE CIVILIZATION

2

PREHISTORY AND THE ORIGINS OF CHINESE CIVILIZATION

1 The Palaeolithic Period

We need say only a few words here about the earliest prehistoric period. Palaeolithic times take us back to such remote epochs that their interest lies more in the history of man as a species than in that of China. We should remember however that in very remote times the eastern slopes of Asia, and, more especially, Yellow River China, were occupied by the ancestors of *homo sapiens*, and also that the great periods of Chinese prehistory run more or less parallel to those of Africa, Europe and Western Asia taken as a whole. Peking Man, or *Sinanthropus*, is one of the most ancient species of hominids known to us, and is estimated to be some 500,000 years old. It would seem that he was able to light fires and that he existed by hunting and living off the wealth of the land. He was probably a cannibal. The *Sinanthropus* was discovered in 1921 in a cave at Chou K'ou Tien near Peking and is now mentioned in every textbook of prehistory. But other finds have been made in China since this date and remains of other specimens of *Sinanthropus* have come to light in Shansi. Some have been dated before Peking Man (discovery made in 1960), and others later (Ting-ts'un Man, 1954).

The existence of a race of giant *Pithecanthropi*, in South

China, who were three to six times larger than a human being and also belonged to the lower Palaeolithic period, was first suspected in 1935 when hominid teeth of exceptional size were found in a chemist's shop in Hong Kong (traditional Chinese pharmacy makes much of 'dragon' bones that appear to be very ancient). These suspicions were confirmed in 1956 and 1957 by the discovery *in situ* in Kwangsi of teeth and fragments of jaw-bones attributed to the same race of giants. The Kwangsi *Gigantopithecus* is closely related to the Javanese *Meganthropus*, and this relationship gives evidence of very ancient links between South China and South East Asia.

The middle and upper Palaeolithic periods are less well represented in China. To the first period belong the discoveries made near Ninghsia in 1922, on the upper reaches of the Yellow River, upstream from the Ordos bend. To the second, the period of the great drought when the loess was formed, belong the finds made in the Ordos (1923) and the vestiges of the upper caves of Chou K'ou Tien (1921-37) where the first *Sinanthropi* were found. More recent discoveries have been made in Szechuan (1951) and Kwangsi (1956).

The Mesolithic period (from 25,000 B.C.?), a transition between the Palaeolithic and Neolithic, is characterized by the appearance of a microlith industry. It is known to us from the excavations carried out in Manchuria in 1926-8, in Kwangsi in 1933, and in Szechuan during the Sino-Japanese war. This period saw the beginning of a climatic differentiation which was to be very important for the history of man in the Far East. In contrast to the wooded valleys of China proper there was now an area of steppes in the region of modern Mongolia or, to borrow Father Teilhard de Chardin's terminology, there was already a contrast between the 'China of loess' and the 'China of sands'. Yellow River China, which was covered by forests and marshland, then had a hot and humid climate which seems to have lasted until the beginnings of the first millennium B.C.

2 The Neolithic Period

(i) *The stages of Neolithic*

We still do not know in which period polished stone was first used in China, or when the first attempts were made at agriculture and stock-breeding. The fourth millennium has sometimes been put forward as a tentative date. It has some likelihood and we may adopt it for the time being.

The most ancient Neolithic cultures arose and developed in the wooded valleys of North China and the Yellow River basin: the valleys of the Wei, the Ching and the upper reaches of the Han in Shensi, Fen valley in Shansi, and the Lo and the middle Yellow River valleys in Honan. They spread towards the east and the west from Kansu as far as Hopei. Hunter-fisher populations still existed and continued to use microliths outside this area to the north, while in the south there were even more backward peoples belonging to the Palaeolithic period. Even at this stage Yellow River China appeared to be ahead of the other regions of eastern Asia and we might also note that the area of Neolithic sites roughly corresponds to the area occupied by the Bronze Age civilization at the end of the second millenium. This, then, was the first sign of a continuity (for which there is other evidence) between the Neolithic periods and the Bronze Age.

Various cultures succeeded each other or coexisted in the Yellow River basin during the period which preceded the birth of Chinese civilization. We may distinguish between them by the state of their agricultural development. The general evolution, which was to continue in the Bronze Age, tended towards permanent forms of agriculture and abode, and towards a relative reduction of the area of cultivated land. The hunter-fisher people who practised a rudimentary form of agriculture as a secondary activity were doubtless succeeded by itinerant farmers who cleared the land by setting fire to the forests and who moved on again when the soil was exhausted. This type of agriculture still survives today in South-east Asia. It is known in Malaya as *ladang* and in Vietnam as *ray* where it is still practised by small groups in the mountain regions (1); there was still some evidence of it in North China at the time of the Western Chou (2). As horticulture and permanent cultivation increased in importance, village communities tended to settle permanently. Social organization then seems to have become more complex and techniques made noticeable progress. It is to these two types (populations of itinerant farmers and settled village communities) that the two major Neolithic cultures in North China seem to belong: one belongs to the Yang Shao (Red Pottery) type, the other to the so-called Lung Shan (Black Pottery) type (3).

(*ii*) *Red Pottery*

In the sites of the first group—now much better known to us thanks to a discovery made near Sian, the capital of Shensi, in 1954—villages were small and only seem to have been inhabited temporarily, sometimes on several occasions. Dwellings were either round or oval holes dug in the ground, with a central hearth, or else circular or rectangular huts built at ground level. Villages also possessed barns, pottery kilns and a cemetery. The nearly circular form of the villages and the position of the dwellings point to a probable clan organization and a system of social classification by age.

Three types of millet were cultivated, including kaoliang, and also perhaps varieties of barley and rice. Tools consisted of hoes, spades, rakes, and round-section axes which were used mainly for clearing the soil. Grain was kept in earthen jars and pounded in a mortar. Hemp and the silk-worm seem to have been known. Pigs and dogs were raised in very large numbers as food; oxen, sheep and rams were fewer.

Very many animals still lived in a wild state, such as the horse, the ox, the rhinoceros, the swamp- and red deer, the leopard, the bamboo rat and the antelope, and hunting remained a primary activity. It was practised by means of traps and snares, spears, javelins, bows and arrows and slings. Fishing also played a great part in the life of these peoples, as is proved by the number of hooks, harpoons and fishing spears and the traces of nets weighted down with stones that have been found. Weapons and implements were made of stone, bone or antler horn. Knives were rectangular and were pierced in the centre or else notched so that they might be fastened to a handle.

The centre of this first group of Neolithic cultures was situated in central Shensi (Wei valley) and in southern Shansi (Fen valley). But they spread out, with certain variations, to the west as far as Kansu and the borders of Chinese Turkestan (Sinkiang), and to the east as far as Shantung. The Yang Shao culture, named after the first of these sites, revealed this early stage of the Chinese Neolithic. It is also known as the Red Pottery culture because of its terracotta vases with ochre bases. Pots were decorated with geometric motifs which curiously resemble those found in the Neolithic centres of the Ukraine and Turkmenistan.

(iii) Black Pottery

Cultures of the Lung Shan type, known as Black Pottery cultures, generally appear to be of later date than the Yang Shao type. But in some places these richer and more highly evolved cultures may have coexisted with the Red Pottery cultures. They centred more in the east, in the modern province of Shantung, spreading towards Honan, southern Hopei and north Kiangsu, and seem related to the Manchurian Neolithic. They are distinct from the Red Pottery cultures in the more durable nature of the settlements; longer occupation of a particular site implies progress in agricultural techniques even though hunting and fishing were still very widely practised by these ancestors of the Chinese. Villages were surrounded by protective walls of pounded earth some twenty feet high and thirty to forty-five feet thick. Dwellings were of the same type as those of the Red Pottery sites but social organization had become more complex. Tombs, of varying degrees of importance, show a marked social differentiation, and religious functions already seem fairly elaborate (traces of agrarian rites, animal sacrifices, miniature vessels no doubt used for funerals, etc.). A new practice appeared, which was to persist in Bronze Age China in the second millennium: divination by means of animal shoulder-blades exposed to fire.

Certain technical peculiarities further distinguish these more evolved cultures from the Red Pottery type. The shape of blades indicates that cutting tools were used more for woodwork than for felling trees, contrary to what had been observed at Yang Shao. Presumably the men of the Black Pottery culture made very great use of wood, like the Chinese of the Shang period, and, like them, also practised the art of wood-engraving. Their pottery was sometimes made on the wheel, with clay of excellent quality, but it was left practically undecorated, perhaps as a result of the development of this art.

(iv) Grey Pottery

The so-called Grey Pottery culture made its appearance in a final stage, immediately preceding the Bronze Age. It is mainly known to us from the sites in Honan where vestiges of it were found immediately below those of the Bronze Age culture, and it seems more closely related to the Bronze Age than to the Black Pottery cultures. The stratigraphy of the Honan sites gives us a highly evocative picture of the succession of cultures right through from the beginning of the Neolithic period to the appearance of bronze. The layers appear in the following order: Shang (beginnings of the Bronze Age)/Hsiao T'un (Grey Pottery)/ Lung Shan (Black Pottery)/ Yang Shao (Red Pottery).

A large number of common features and analogies between the last Neolithic cultures and the beginnings of the Bronze Age gives evidence of a continuous evolution: persistence of the same type of knife, semi-subterranean dwellings, divination by fire, tripod vases whose stylistic evolution may be followed from the period of Black Pottery up to the bronze cast models of the late second millennium and beyond, persistence of the same Mongoloid human type characterized by spade-shaped incisors. In addition, the most recent discoveries bear out the fact that the beginnings of Bronze Age civilization show very little progress compared to the already advanced Neolithic cultures of Lung Shan and the Grey Pottery cultures. All this leads us to conclude that Chinese traditions relating to the remotest archaic period are not entirely devoid of foundation. Accordingly the Hsia dynasty, traditionally dated to the late third and early second millennium B.C., which precedes that of the Shang, may well correspond to a late Neolithic culture which already possessed a rudimentary form of political organization. Possibly certain sites in south Shansi and Honan may one day be found to be related to this Chinese 'dynasty' preceeding the Bronze Age.

3 Origins of the Bronze Age Civilization

Most recent discoveries seem to suggest a gradual transition from polished stone to bronze rather than a brutal rupture between one epoch and the next. This was inconceivable before the Second World War. The Chinese Neolithic was then much less familiar than it is today, and the discoveries at Anyang had revealed a Bronze Age civilization whose antecedents were entirely unknown. Bronze techniques were so highly perfected at Anyang (fourteenth–eleventh century) that some scholars thought this artistry must have been imported into northern China in the second millennium. But, since 1952, excavations have uncovered Shang sites of earlier date than Anyang. The few bronze pieces found there are thin, and decorated in the most rudimentary fashion. They consist largely of tools and weapons (mainly knives and arrow-heads). However, these sites have also revealed other archaic features. As in the Neolithic periods, dwellings were partly sunk below ground-level. They are rectangular pits sometimes reinforced by walls of pounded earth. The flat bones used for divination by fire were still crudely prepared.

It would seem then that, like bronze techniques, the other arts such as architecture, pottery, wood-engraving, astronomy, divination and religious practices were perfected rather slowly between the beginnings of the Bronze Age and the last centuries of the second millennium. There can no longer be any doubt that it was in China that the art of bronze was born. It only took the ancient Chinese a few centuries to attain the highest degree of mastery in the art, as proved by the pieces found at Anyang; this suggests that the beginnings of the Bronze Age may perhaps have coincided with those of the Shang dynasty, or else only just preceded them. It is possible that the discovery of bronze in China dates from about 1700 B.C., give or take a century. Now, we should also bear in mind that it was precisely in the eighteenth century B.C. that the Shang dynasty came to power, according to Chinese tradition (4).

We must therefore reject the hypothesis of an invasion and a process of borrowing, and allow that bronze techniques originated in China itself; but it does not necessarily follow that this birth was entirely spontaneous. Remote influences must have played some part in the appearance of the technique in Yellow River China. From the Neolithic period onwards, the painted pottery of Yang Shao brings proof of relations between this region and the countries near the Caspian Sea. The middle Yellow River region was situated at a cross-roads and was always open to remote influences from Siberia and the oases of Central Asia. In the case of bronze, we naturally think of the place where the earliest evidence of the art of alloying was found: it would have been transmitted to northern China by the peoples of the steppes, who themselves must have received the technique from Mesopotamia, or rather the regions of southern Russia into which this productive idea spread from its original birthplace.

There exist traces of remote influences and relations even for the Shang period. Certain forms of Shang pottery have been found at Djemet-Nasr and at Mohenjo-Daro in the north-west of the Indian subcontinent. The jades found at Anyang were no doubt imported from Central Asia, as were those of later periods. Certain animal motifs are curiously reminiscent of those of Mesopotamia, with their serpents with interlacing tails, tigers and other animals confronting one another and framing a human figure as on the Lion Gate in ancient Mycenae. From the same regions (Chinese Turkestan, Transoxiana, Iran and north-west India) artistic and intellectual influences were to come during the most brilliant periods of Chinese history. From the Han to the T'ang, Chinese music, sculpture, games, folk-lore, and religion were to owe much to contributions from these regions. Until the twelfth century, the Chinese capital cities with their cosmopolitan populations were to remain in the fertile plains of the middle Yellow River where the Bronze civilization had first developed. They formed a cross-roads: to the north and north-west lay the Mongol steppes and the oases of Central Asia, and to the south the Yangtse valley.

From the Shang period onwards, this region was also in touch with South China and the countries of South-east Asia. The giant tortoises, whose ventral carapaces were used for divination in the late second millennium, were probably offered as tribute by the peoples of the Yangtse valley, or else may have come from Malaya. The cowrie shells which served as objects of value to the Shang and the Western Chou, could have been imported from Burma or the Maldives. Also from the south came at least some of the tin necessary for bronze casting, in the shape of ingots. Certain Shang bronzes on which were represented Melan-esian or negroid human types (large, round faces with flattened noses) also confirm the existence of relations between Shang China and the countries of South-east Asia (5). To conclude, we should point out that it has been possible to compare the animal engravings of the Shang and Chou periods with the engravings on the totem poles found on the north-west coast of North America. Striking analogies in motifs and composition suggest that there were relations between archaic China and North America by way of the Behring Straits (6).

Everything then leads us to a conclusion in which facts retain their full value and apparently contradictory evidence is reconciled: from its very beginnings, the originality of Chinese civilization never excluded a variety of outside influences. This conclusion applies to the whole of Chinese history.

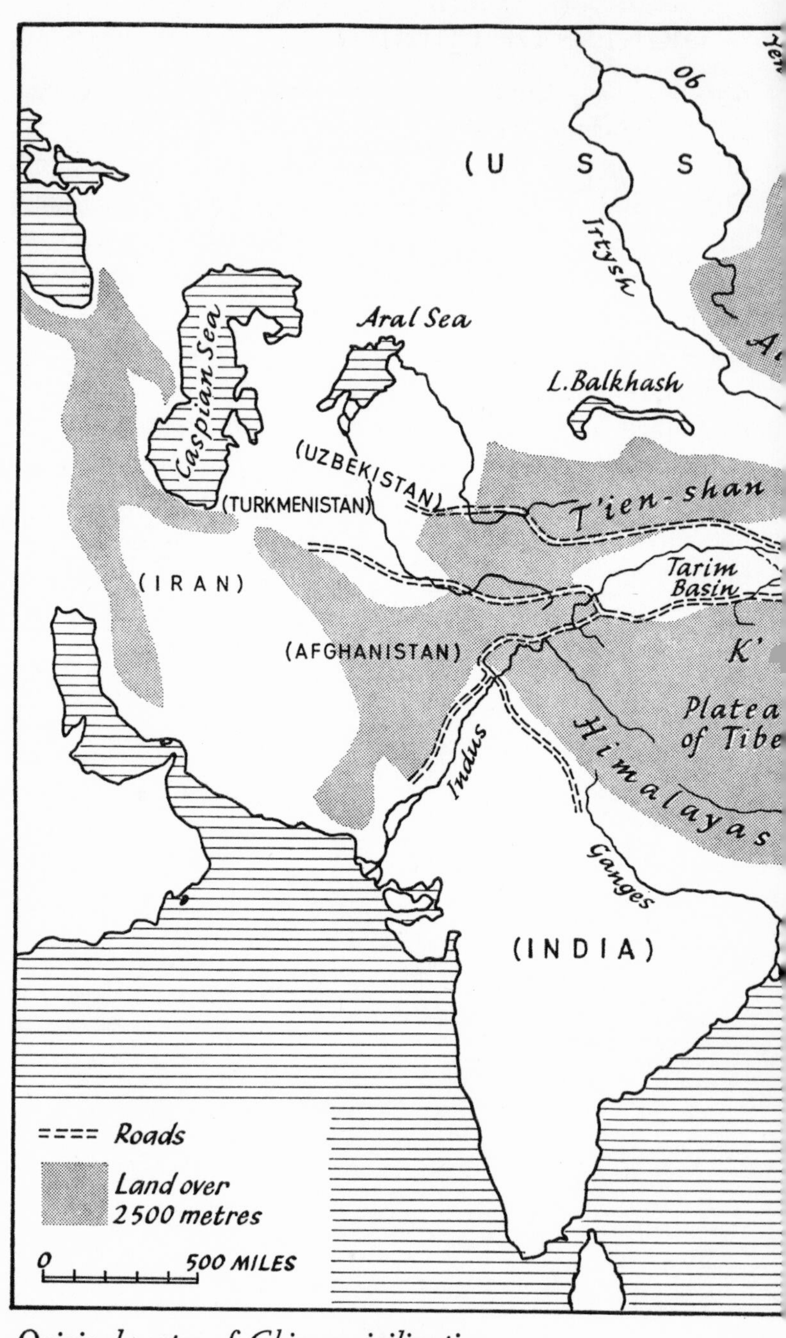

Original centre of Chinese civilization

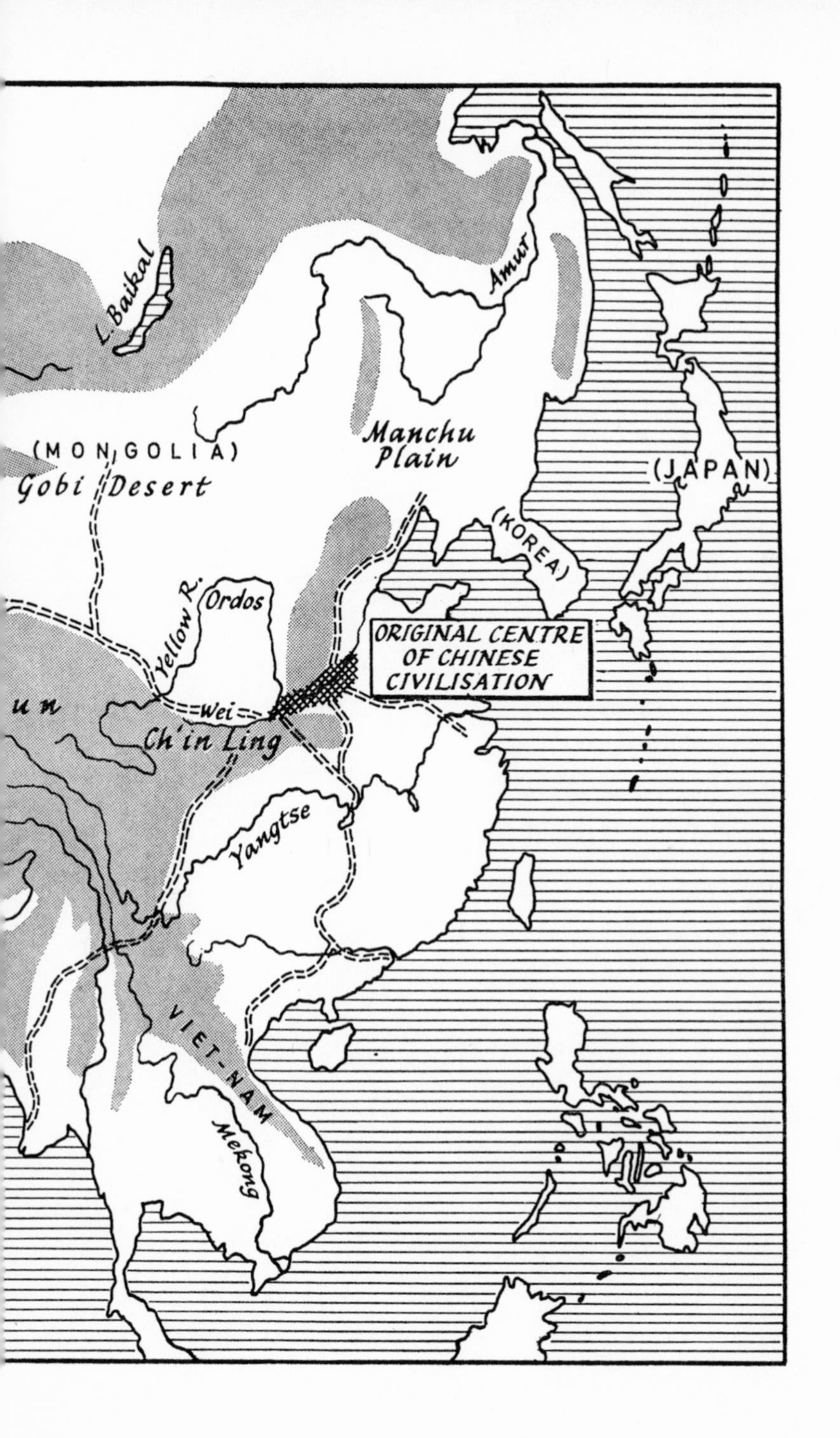

L. Baikal
Amur
Manchu Plain
(MONGOLIA)
Gobi Desert
(JAPAN)
(KOREA)
Yellow R.
Ordos
ORIGINAL CENTRE OF CHINESE CIVILISATION
un
Wei
Ch'in Ling
Yangtse
VIET-NAM
Mekong

THE ARCHAIC PERIOD

3

THE ARCHAIC PERIOD

The Shang and the Western Chou [18th? to 8th Century BC]

1 Economy and Society

(*i*) *Early dualism in Chinese society*

The discovery of bronze-casting seems to have had a decisive effect during the formative period of Chinese civilization. We may be sure that there was some continuity between the end of the Neolithic Age and the Bronze Age; and the Grey Pottery culture must certainly be considered as a proto-Chinese culture. But Chinese civilization—with all its most characteristic features—began with the discovery of bronze. Bronze-casting brought with it on the one hand a number of highly important technical innovations such as horse-drawn chariots, writing, calendars, and new architectural forms, and, on the other, a social dichotomy that was to be of vital importance for Chinese history, by which society was divided into townsfolk (warrior noblemen and hunters) and the peasantry. The most recent archaeological discoveries have confirmed Marcel Granet's intuitions in about 1925, when, after nothing but a careful analysis of fragments of legends and mythological themes, he wrote: 'If (our) conclusions are right we could date the foundation of military districts and towns, the establishment of a feudal and military régime, and the division of rural communities into groups of villagers and city-dwellers, with the aid of a chronology for the history of techniques. We might then conclude that the *crystallizing factor* had been the appearance of bronze-work and the bronze trade in China.' (1)

It would appear that the coexistence of complementary village and town populations was one of the earliest formative features of Chinese civilization. The first Bronze Age towns were founded on sites which had been cleared in Neolithic times. From the very beginning, the discovery of alloys must have led to a specialization of functions. The rural populations who had formerly devoted themselves to hunting and agriculture—activities that may have been divided between the sexes—began to concentrate almost exclusively on agriculture once they were assured of the protection of the inhabitants of the aristocratic towns who became mostly warriors and hunters—the affinities between hunting and warfare being both numerous and clear in archaic China.

(ii) Place of agriculture in archaic Chinese economy

This very old social dualism leads to the following question which has aroused great controversy: what place did agriculture have in the China of the Shang period? For a long time, the traditional belief was that Chinese civilization—perfect from the very beginning—had been almost exclusively agricultural, even in its earliest periods. In fact it was only much later, during the last five hundred years before the Christian era, that North China and the Yangtse valley became a vast, densely populated area that was continuously farmed. The development of a state structure, unknown in the archaic periods, had been necessary for this to happen, likewise the diffusion of the new iron-casting technique. At the end of the second millennium, Yellow River China was quite unlike what it became at the beginning of the Empire. All the available evidence shows a country still covered by great forests and vast marshes, with an astonishing number of birds, fish, and game of every size, including a great many deer of all species, tigers, wild oxen, bears, boars and wild cats, not to mention wolves, foxes, monkeys and every kind of small game. A large number of wild beasts were captured or killed in the great royal hunts; the larger game such as deer and boars was counted in tens. One inscription mentions 348 deer slain in a single hunt. But in the Shang period the Yellow River basin was also inhabited by animals it is unusual to find at such a high altitude, elephants, rhinoceros, buffaloes, panthers, antelopes, leopards and tapirs. Both the inscriptions found on the site at Anyang, and the animal bones that have been unearthed prove the existence of tropical or subtropical fauna.

The picture of the northern plain in the ninth to eighth centuries given by the ancient poems of the *Shih Ching* shows it as not very different from during the Shang period. It was still covered largely by marshes and forests of small trees (plum-trees, elms, wild pear-trees, willows, chestnuts and cypresses) and there were many fruit-bearing plants. Game was still extremely abundant and there were few further signs of human settlement.

The richness of the fauna and flora makes it certain that archaic China was sparsely inhabited. Since there were also animals from tropical regions it is probably true that the climate of North China in the late second and early first millennium was much gentler and more humid than today. Progress in land-clearing resulted in a drier and colder climate. In any case, from the fifth to the third centuries B.C., North China had a very different natural equilibrium.

As in the Lung Shan and Grey Pottery cultures the Shang people used a great deal of wood for their buildings and vessels. A whole series of bronze vases with angular forms would seem to be copies of wooden vases. Moreover, Shang art was zoomorphic, not only in decoration but also in form. In this respect it displays astonishing imaginativeness and inventive genius (vases took the form of sheep, owl, rhinoceros or elephant). By its art alone, the Chinese civilization of the Shang period seems to have been far more a civilization of hunters and foresters than of farmers.

Finally, the raising of cattle, oxen and horses for drawing chariots must have been a very important activity. Traces exist of ancient dances which seem to have been peculiar to brotherhoods of cattle-breeders (**2**) and there are inscriptions which very often mention sacrifices of several dozen sheep and oxen.

All these considerations lead us to limit the importance of agriculture in the economy of archaic China. The originality of early Chinese civilization was certainly not due to agriculture, which was already known and practised in the fertile lands of the Yellow River basin in the Neolithic period, but rather to all the innovations that may be ascribed to the noble classes of the walled cities. This view is confirmed by the fact that agricultural implements of the time were still of a rudimentary nature. The implements of peasants in the Shang period were very similar to those of the proto-Chinese of the Black Pottery cultures: stone hoes, wooden spades with two teeth, knives of oval or half-moon shape, usually in schist and sometimes in bivalve shell. The cereals they chose to use were sorghum, a variety of barley, two kinds of millet (yellow and black) and a kind of hemp with edible seeds. They raised the same domestic animals as the peoples of the Yang Shao and Lung Shan cultures: pigs, dogs and poultry. Lastly, if we are to believe the literary evidence of the Western Chou period, fresh-water fishing, the hunting of small game, herb and wild fruit picking made up an important part of the diet of the peasantry.

It is clear therefore that the growing of cereals in the China of the late second and early first millennium was a far less important activity than it became in the fourth to third centuries B.C. On the contrary, what strikes us in the archaic period is the great variety of resources and the diversity of the economy.

(*iii*) *Heterogeneous character of archaic society*

Such a varied economy might lead us to the *a priori* conclusion that there was a relative diversity of society; history confirms this. Neither the town nobility nor the country folk seem to show any sign of homogeneity.

First it must be noted that the Chinese were surrounded by Barbarians, i.e. unassimilated or only partially assimilated peoples (3). But since these peoples were usually in such close contact with the Chinese that they seem to form part of them, they cannot be considered separately. Frequent raids and punitive expeditions, and exchanges of goods and wives gradually integrated these Barbarians into the Chinese world. In a general manner, the influence of the palace-city decreased with distance, and the ancient Chinese were aware of this decline of civilizing influence in proportion to distance. Beyond the neighbouring areas which formed part of the city's territory lived the Barbarians who had been subdued and were now allies; farther away, no doubt, were other Barbarians with whom the Chinese had only sporadic contact, and even farther away were almost unknown peoples whom the ancient Chinese saw as monsters and compared to wild beasts.

During this ceaseless process of fusion with neighbouring peoples, marriage alliances enriched and renewed the town nobility with their constant contributions, and warlike expeditions must certainly have added to the population. It is possible that prisoners of war formed a relatively important part of the lower classes in archaic China and also that there was a slow transformation of Barbarians into Chinese even within the city territories.

More generally, the diversity of occupations seems to have determined a variety of social status reflected in the vocabulary of the time. Stock-breeders and shepherds, slaves employed to look after horses, town craftsmen (potters, chariot-makers, blacksmiths), all seem to have formed as many distinct groups as there were varied degrees of servitude. And, no doubt, not even the farmers formed a uniform group.

(*iv*) *The peasantry*

The farmers represented only a part of the lower classes but seem to have been the most important group and the one that was to develop most.

Although the techniques of the farmers of the Shang period hardly differed from those of their Neolithic ancestors, the closeness of the palace-city completely modified living conditions. Living as they did under the religious and military protection of the city this peasantry was confined by social conditions to specialized activities like agriculture and breeding domestic animals. Products such as cereals, wine, pigs and edible dogs was used for the sacrifices of the noble class. Sacrifices of pigs, in particular, as mentioned in the divinatory inscriptions of Anyang, seem to have been very numerous. The royal power took great interest in future harvests and weather conditions, which were always uncertain and therefore could seriously affect crops. Actually, the royal power had its own dealings with the heavens. But this solicitude can also be explained by the fact that religious rites required a very abundant use of alcoholic beverages, and not perhaps because the noble classes—carnivorous by preference—consumed many cereals. Moreover, in the Chou period at least, details of farming were decided by rural inspectors. Their main duty was to settle boundaries, and later authors might be wrong in considering the inspectors real agronomists. At a time when the fertile lands of North China were still sparsely populated the question of the distribution of land between various types of cultivation, pasture lands and hunting domains must have been far more urgent than the improvement of yields.

Besides, there were few problems of land ownership in the archaic periods. The only known form of landed holding was the fief, defined as a religious and military domination over an area of land, limited by raised banks of ditches (*feng*) (4). In this context, deliveries of cereals, beverages and breeding animals appear to have assumed a religious character; goods which embodied the virtues of the land were destined for sacrifice and were not fit for consumption until they had been blessed. Economics as such were as yet unknown, and relations between men had not yet acquired the abstract character they assumed with the diffusion of currency and the use of contracts.

Documents of a relatively late date seem to suggest a strict division of functions and activities between the sexes in the peasant world of the Chou period, and no doubt in that of the Shang as well. Weaving, silk-worm culture, and wine-making were a woman's domain whereas work in the fields, harvesting, small game hunting and fishing were masculine activities. It is likely that this division of functions and collaboration between the sexes were the source of certain extremely persistent images in Chinese thought. The opposition between male and female manifested itself on temporal and spatial levels: indoor and outdoor life and the peasant dwelling, the season of work in the fields and winter inactivity, places exposed to the sun and those in the shade. All these opposing but complementary realities depended on the two general principles of the *yin* (manner of being and feminine powers) and the *yang* (manner of being and masculine powers).

The peasantry lived in great families with their own system of classifying relationships (no distinction was made between the father and paternal uncles and they formed part of one group; the same applied to the mother and maternal aunts). The most frequent type of marriage was between crossed cousins, the man marrying the daughter of the maternal uncle, which meant that wives were chosen, in preference, from among the mother's family. At the time of the *Shih Ching* poems, the girls usually came to settle in their husband's village but there is evidence to suggest that fosterage (the practice by which the future son-in-law was raised by his maternal uncles) was much more frequent in the early period.

The whole of peasant life was ruled by the clear-cut distinction between the winter period of rest and the season of agricultural work, with festivities to mark the beginning and end of each. The spring festivals seem to have been the occasion for competitions between the sexes, with groups of boys and girls from different villages singing and dancing in turn. They occurred in holy places, often at the junction of rivers where ancestral spirits roamed in readiness for reincarnation (5).

(v) The noble class

It is likely that the founders of the first Bronze Age towns were the heads of brotherhoods of bronze-casters, although other groups (hunters and livestock-breeders) must have contributed towards forming the city nobility.

But what was a town in archaic times? Above all it was a palace surrounded by pounded earth walls which protected the inhabitants from both invasions and floods. The towns were generally built near a river. The ramparts, some twenty-five feet high and thirty to fifty feet thick, formed a square or rectangle orientated according to the four cardinal points, with gateways on each side. This pattern remained traditional in China until the modern period and, originally, must have been connected with ritual practices for regulating the seasons and the motions of the sun. The gateways were holy for through them good or bad influences penetrated into the city and misfortunes were driven out.

The Shang and Chou towns covered very small areas. Excavations have shown that the last capital of the Shang, the largest town of its time, measured no more that 800 yards in perimeter. The rituals of the late Chou record a tradition, doubtless already valid in the Shang period, that the king's residence (and similarly that of the lords which had the same layout) was orientated on a north-south axis and contained three successive courtyards. To the north of the central courtyard and facing south lay the audience chamber, some three steps above ground-level, where the prince would stand during ritual ceremonies. All the buildings were rectangular, with a double sloping roof supported by wooden pillars, and stood on the platforms characteristic of public buildings in China. To the east of this courtyard lay the temple of the ancestors and, to the west, the altar of the Earth (called earth-god by the Chou). Ancestors and earth-gods were differently oriented and had opposite functions; the ancestors generally granted good fortune, the earth-god was a punitive, malignant divinity. Captives and perjurers were executed on the altar of the earth-god and armies setting off on a campaign took a vow before it, pledging themselves unto death.

The central courtyard was the holy place *par excellence* and in the capital it was regarded as the centre of the world. Here, in the presence of the ancestors and the earth-god, took place all the ritual acts, recalled for us by inscriptions on the bronze vessels of the Chou period; they included investitures, orders, donations and judgments during which each of the participants occupied a prearranged place on one of the four sides of the courtyard.

North of the prince's residence lay the market. South of it lived the craftsmen on whom the nobility depended for fighting and hunting; they were chariot-makers, arrow-makers, bow-makers, armourers, blacksmiths and potters. The south of town was also the home of various officials of the noble rule, such as stewards, scribes, diviners, and directors of rituals.

The whole life of the archaic city was centred round the palace, and commercial and manufacturing activities were totally dependent on this religious and military centre. The term palace-city therefore provides a useful definition.

The Chinese world of the archaic period was composed of a number of walled cities which were both religious and military centres and which served as residences for the nobility. The royal capital and the towns of vassals, related to the king either by blood or alliance, lay scattered throughout Yellow River China in the midst of more or less assimilated Barbarian populations. Each palace-city was a copy of the capital and formed an identical unity, for there was the same general layout of buildings, the same administrative organization, and the same kind of relation between, on the one hand, the city-dwellers and country farmers, on the other, the Barbarian chiefdoms. The centre of the Shang domain was in eastern and north-eastern Honan, and palace-cities seem to have been most numerous in the area corresponding to the modern province of Honan and southern Hopei. In the south-east their domain stretched as far as the Huai valley, and to Shantung in the east. But it would seem that Chinese influence reached even farther afield at the end of the second millennium. In the west, it reached as far as the Wei valley in Shensi, and from there it penetrated to the south of Kansu and the Chengtu plain in Szechuan. In the south it seems that it had already reached the region of the middle Yangtse (6) along the Han valley.

The noble classes were graded in a rigid hierarchy in the Chou period. They formed a pyramid with the king, as holder of the most important religious privileges, at the apex, and the families of mere gentlemen, who provided the majority of warriors, at the base. The lords, heads of the city, were invested by the king. Relatively late texts mention a kind of *per glebam* investiture by which the vassal received a lump of earth taken from the altar of the royal earth-god on the side corresponding to the orientation of the fief and the particular colour connected with this direction (7). Below the king and the princes came the heads of the great noble families who held posts at court and constituted a kind of grand vizir class. Next came the families of barons who lived on the revenue of the lands of the villages they

KANSU
Northern Lo
Fen
SHANS
3
Anyan
Wei
4
3?
8
Loyang
Sian
2
SHENSI
HO
Han
SZECHUAN
HU
Minkiang
Yangtse
HUNAN
Districts where Shang-style sites have been discovered
3 Number of sites
Borders of provinces

Shang sites

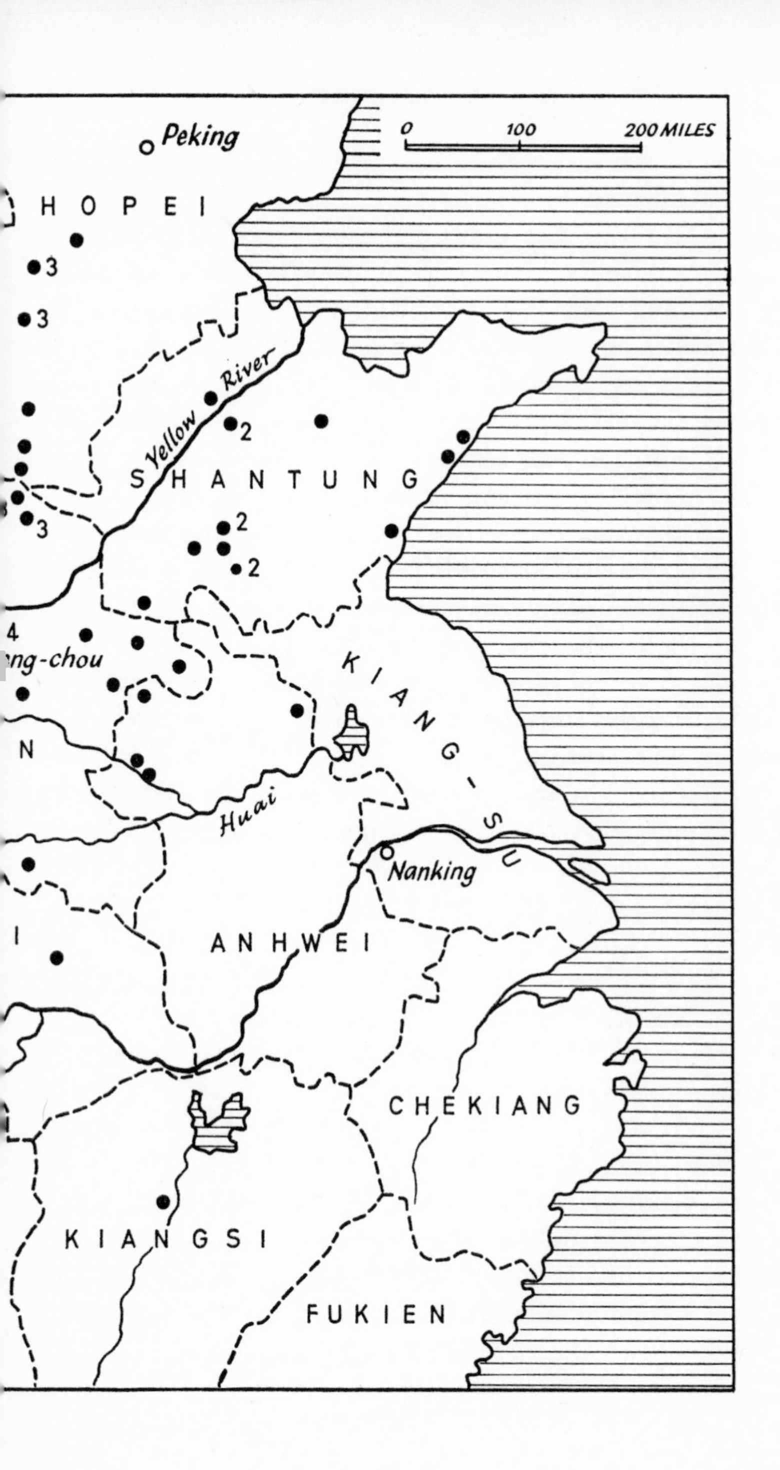
Peking
0
100
200 MILES
HOPEI
Yellow River
SHANTUNG
KIANG-SU
Huai
Nanking
ANHWEI
CHEKIANG
KIANGSI
FUKIEN

had been given, and finally after the barons, the class of plain gentlemen.

The vassal princes sometimes took part in the wars and great royal hunts, each providing their own contingent of chariots and warriors. They also received the king during his travels, supplied labour for the royal palace, and gave tributes consisting of sacrificial animals, tortoise-shells, copper, tin, and cowrie shells. In return, the king backed his vassals with his own armed force. Similar exchanges were fixed between princes and barons.

The administration of the Shang and Chou towns was bound up with the way of life of the noble class, and therefore consisted mainly of domestic, religious and military functions. In the Shang period, 'functionaries' were appointed in charge of horses and chariots, bows and arrows, lances, shields, dogs, chiefs of guards, diviners, invokers, scribes, etc. In the Chou period, the number of these officials tended to increase and the administrators of the rural populations must have become more important as land-clearing (**8**) made progress.

(*vi*) *Life of the noble class*

Apart from its religious activities, the noble class devoted its time to hunting and warfare. In the archaic period no distinction was made between the two. The weapons used were the same, and great hunting parties were useful for training troops. Even the assembly places were the same. Captives and game were treated identically and consecrated to the ancestors and the gods. Some of the prisoners were, in fact, executed at the moment of triumph, or else kept in reserve as sacrificial offerings. Thus, according to an inscription at Anyang, three sheep, thirty oxen and two prisoners were sacrificed to a defunct queen on the counsel of a diviner. Warfare was directed against rebellious towns or barbarians and more resembled raids since the aim was not to conquer new territories but to acquire precious goods, farmers, slaves, craftsmen, animals for breeding, and crops.

Weapons included various types of bows using pellets and arrows, including a very powerful reflex bow peculiar to eastern and northern Asia, and a dagger-axe set in a long handle, found only in archaic China and used for hooking the enemy's weapon and striking the first blow. It was transformed into a halberd in the course of time. Lances, hatchets, helmets, shields and cuirasses bring this list of weapons to an end (9).

The chariot was used in warfare until the third century B.C., but it was to lose its importance from the late sixth century B.C. as infantry took over. It was a light carriage with two wheels and a shaft. The rider's box was square or rectangular, had railings, and was covered by a circular dais (a square surmounted by a circle symbolizing the earth covered by the sky). It was drawn by two horses although sometimes an additional pair might be harnessed to loose traces on either side of the main pair. Three men rode in the chariot: the driver in the centre, an archer on the left and a lancer on the right (10).

The nobles formed the core of the army. They alone possessed chariots and horses, and they alone had effective weapons. The rest of the army was made up of valets, carriers and grooms. Most of these foot-soldiers (*t'u*) must have been recruited from among the peasantry. In the Shang period, when chariots were grouped by units of five and larger formations of twenty-five, expeditions were usually made up of some thousands of ordinary soldiers and over a hundred chariots.

The marching troops were regulated like a ballet by bells and drums, and their ornamentation and colours give evidence of the importance attached to the psychological aspects of warfare; the military expedition was quite as much a deployment of magico-religious forces as of positive physical force.

(vii) History

We have little exact information on the political history of China in the Shang and Western Chou periods. During the centuries before the capital was established at Anyang, the Shang seem to have changed their capital seven times, in north and north-east Honan, and south and north of the present course of the Yellow River. Recent excavations have partly confirmed this tradition, for the sites of Cheng Chou and Yen Shih, the east of Loyang, correspond to those of capitals previous to the Anyang period (fourteenth–eleventh century). Moreover, the study of divinatory inscriptions on oracle bones and tortoise-shells has allowed scholars to reconstitute the list of the thirty Shang kings. This list is almost identical to the one which the historian Ssu-ma Ch'ien (163–85 B.C.) had obtained from a tradition dating back a thousand years. In it, we find only three cases of inversion between two consecutive kings and only two incorrect filiations. Among the first thirteen rulers, the normal mode of succession was from elder brother to younger brother, for the son only succeeded in exceptional cases. But in the case of the last four kings, succession from father to son became the rule, and was to persist in later periods.

During the last period, when the capital was set up near Anyang, the Shang very frequently seem to have made war on the peoples who lived in the Huai valley and who had so far escaped assimilation. These battles may explain why it was that the Chou—a Chinese principality greatly influenced by local populations and whose centre lay north of the Wei valley in Shensi—so easily seized the capital at the end of the twelfth century (or more probably, at the beginning of the eleventh), and were able to take the place of the Shang. From then onwards, the capital of the Chinese world was to be situated on the site of modern Sian in the centre of the Wei basin, and a secondary capital was to be built near modern Loyang in Honan. The remarkable thing is that these two sites were later to be capitals of the Han (206 B.C.–A.D. 220) and T'ang (618–907) dynasties.

Bronze inscriptions are our main source of information for the period of the Western Chou; but these texts tell us more about institutions than political history. For this period, we have at least the list of names of those kings who inspired more or less legendary traditions. The only definite, important historical fact we possess is the invasion of the Shensi Barbarians towards the middle of the eighth century B.C., which forced the Chou to take refuge in Honan under the protection of the principality of Cheng, and to take up permanent residence at Loyang. Thenceforth, the power and prestige of the house of Chou was to diminish rapidly and entirely new historical developments were to take place.

2 The Mental Universe

(*i*) *Rites and religious concepts*

We are aware of the importance of ritual in China. By ritual we mean that regulation of deeds and activities that was so intimately linked with cosmological conceptions. It follows that the regulation was not regarded as an arbitrary convention, but on the contrary as being in harmony with the cycle of the seasons, the motion of heavenly bodies and the special powers of the cosmic directions. No doubt it derived its powers of suggestion from this conviction. However, this system of constraints must have evolved slowly. What we know of the behaviour of the men of the Shang periods suggest that it had not evolved fully at the end of the second millennium. The excesses traditionally imputed to the last Shang sovereign surely correspond to historical fact, and the excavations at Anyang have proved to what extent the last kings of this dynasty were unfamiliar with the virtues of moderation. Theirs was a world of luxury and violence. Enormous wealth (livestock, metals, agricultural produce, game, and prisoners of war) was set apart for ritual purposes and nearly all the goods that this society possessed were lavished on routine or exceptional sacrifices, or on the funerals of kings and great noblemen. Sheep, oxen, pigs, dogs and deer were sacrificed by the dozen. Offerings of thirty or forty oxen to a single ancestor were by no means the exception and there were distinctive characters to designate sacrifices of one hundred oxen, one hundred pigs, ten white pigs, ten oxen and ten sheep. The victims could be decapitated or have their throats slit; they could be smoked or roasted, quartered and offered up cooked or raw, whole or in sections. Sometimes they were buried in the ground, thrown in the water or burnt. It follows that sometimes food was consumed and wealth redistributed, and sometimes there was destruction pure and simple. In the first case, gods and men, ancestors and the living all feasted together in banquets which must certainly have become orgies for there was an abundance of victuals and alcoholic beverages. In the Chou period, the Shang had the reputation of drunkards. They may well have deserved it for beakers designed specially for alcoholic drinks take pride of place among Shang bronze and pottery vessels.

Although control of expenditure was not yet necessary in a world in which hunting and stock-breeding seem to have provided more than enough food, certain very ancient factors, already present in the Shang period, may have contributed to the forming of the system of rituals. From the start the Chinese, founders of walled cities, probably set enormous value on the position of the stars and orientations when building palace-cities, in the disposition of neighbouring territories, in sacred ceremonies and court dances. We may already discern an elementary cosmic system in which sacred acts were not only an expression of the universal order but the very principle on which its realization depended. Mimed dramas, animal or masked dances, whose traces Marcel Granet has endeavoured to find, appear as descriptions of the ordering of the world. They had the virtue of recreating the royal power anew, or inaugurating a new age, and of organizing the space surrounding the city into four separate sectors. By observing the heavens the Chinese must certainly have found material for a royal system of symbols at an early stage. The first mode of governing may well have been an imitation of the movements of the heavens. From the Shang period on the king was known as the son of Heaven (or perhaps, 'prince holding a fief from the heavens'). The celestial world was a replica of the terrestrial world. Like the Shang king, the god of the Heavens, the 'Sovereign-on-high' had his vassals who included ancestors of the royal family, the gods of the wind, the clouds, the sun and the moon and the stars, one of the most important being the so-called bird-constellation in the southern heavens that was later to become the Red Bird. These celestial deities did not accept offerings but were contacted through the intermediary of the royal ancestors (11).

The Sovereign-on-high protected towns, presided over their foundation, assured victory in war, brought rain, wind, drought, and misfortunes to the earth. But this divinity who intervened in the world of mankind seems to have gradually lost his individuality as agricultural activities began to predominate. Writers in the last three centuries before the Empire tended to see Heaven as nothing more than nature and inherent cosmic order.

We may detect the outlines of a certain world order in the religious concepts of the Shang; the divinities-on-high, and ancestors and celestial gods had their counterparts in the gods of the earth—doubtless already hierarchized—the gods who presided over the four sectors surrounding the capital city, and those of certain rivers and mountains (the most important deity being that of the Yellow River to whom it was already the custom, as it was to be under the Chou, to offer young maidens in marriage). Earth and river and mountain gods were to remain an important object of worship in later epochs. Should we deduce a social dichotomy from these two very different categories of divine powers? The earth gods of the peasants and conquered and assimilated barbarians would seem to have joined up with the gods of the nobles who had founded the towns.

(ii) *Ancestor worship*

The worship of royal ancestors was a central part of the religion of the Shang and the Chou. Their funerary tablets—which represented their souls—were kept in front of the temple of the ancestors in stone urns, which meant in effect that all rituals were carried out in the ancestors' presence.

Every great event in the life of the royal family and all the solemnities of the Court were announced aloud to them. The ancestors served other religious powers as mediators and intervened in the private life of the royal family, appearing in their dreams, sending illnesses and influencing harvests. They were frequently consulted by diviners. Shoulder-blades of sheep or oxen or the ventral parts of tortoise-shells into which small cavities had been bored were heated, and the shape of the resulting cracks enabled the diviner to interpret the answers of the ancestor consulted. In the Shang period, this divinatory rite (which has been studied by a college of specialists so that today we know the names of more than a hundred Shang diviners) usually seems to have been preceded by a sacrifice which was intended to obtain the good will of the ancestors. A large number of objects used for divination by fire have been found at Anyang and a few in other sites such as Cheng Chou and Loyang, in Honan, and the Sian region in Shensi. A small number are inscribed with the questions put to the ancestors, and in some cases, with their answers. So far, 41,000 inscribed pieces have been published, and of the 3,000 characters found on them more than 1,000 have been identified successfully (**12**). We owe all we know of Shang civilization between the mid-fourteenth and the eleventh century to the patient deciphering of these inscriptions undertaken since 1899 and, above all, to the work of three great Chinese scholars who must be mentioned here: Lo Chen-yü, Wang Kuo-wei and Tung Tso-pin. Thanks to the study of these inscriptions we know that the questions put to the ancestors concerned the sacrifices they demanded, natural phenomena, agriculture, stock-breeding, military expeditions, the private affairs of the king's household (hunts, journeys, dreams, illnesses, births) or else the lucky or unlucky nature of the next ten days to come. We also know that the cyclic sign which designated each ancestor-king corresponded to the day on which it was customary to offer him sacrifices; the ten days of the 'week' were named after a series of ten special signs. Only the sovereigns of the main branch were venerated, together with their queens, unlike the ancestors of the collateral branches. The Shang kings were in fact polygamous and could have numerous secondary wives, but there might equally be several queens.

Since 1950 the discovery and systematic excavation of the great royal tombs at Anyang have greatly increased our knowledge of funerary customs at the end of the Shang period. These tombs appear as rectangular pits with four ramps leading to them from the north, south, east and west, and a central shaft (the ramps constituted a royal privilege according to the rituals of a later period). They are few in number and differ from the less important tombs in the greater complexity of their architecture and the abundance of their funerary furnishings. It is only in these tombs that bronzes have been found. By contrast the ordinary tombs contain only pottery vessels, and the smallest are quite bare. The furnishings of the royal tombs are remarkable for their great luxury, and include a series of bronze bells and musical stones, which enable us to know the musical scale in use in this period, various types of bronze ritual vases, weapons, pottery, horse-drawn chariots at the north and south issues, and a dog buried in a small grave underneath the coffin.

But above all, the excavations that have been reopened at Anyang since 1950 have strikingly confirmed the practice of human sacrifice: the number of men who were destined to follow their kings into the next world is surprisingly high. In one tomb alone, and its ancillary parts, more than 300 skeletons have been found, some intact, others decapitated. The kings seem to have been surrounded in their tombs by their suite, queens and concubines, guards, coachmen, huntsmen and various officials. Almost a thousand years later the Chinese writer Mo-tzu recalled these sumptuary customs and human sacrifices which had not entirely disappeared by his time: 'On the death of a prince, the store-houses and treasuries are emptied. Gold, jade, and pearls are placed on the body. Rolls of silk and chariots with their horses are buried in the grave. But an abundance of hangings are also needed for the funerary chamber, as well as tripod vases, drums, tables, pots, ice containers, war-axes, swords, plumed standards, ivories and animal skins. No one is satisfied unless all these riches accompany the deceased. As for the men who are sacrificed so they may follow him, if he should be a son of Heaven, they will be counted in hundreds or tens. If he is a great officer or a baron, they will be counted in tens or units.' There is other written evidence for the time between the end of the archaic period and the Empire, and excavations have also proved that this practice was continued. But these human sacrifices which sometimes seem to have been of a voluntary nature, gradually diminished in the course of the first millennium and occurred only sporadically during the Empire (13). The economic, political, and social evolution of the Chinese world from the end of the archaic period onwards must certainly be the explanation for the reprobation these sacrificial murders provoked. It would seem that the limiting of expenses for economic reasons and the ritual and moral rule of moderation were connected in their development. At the end of the archaic period it became the custom to replace human victims by wicker figures or life-size statues in wood or terracotta. From the beginning of the Empire, they became no more than small pottery figurines (and later paper objects which were burned at the moment of the funeral). From the Han to the T'ang periods, tombs have yielded a very large number of these miniature images and many examples are now on show in museums. They include models of furniture, houses, stables, wells, domestic animals, and various personages such as musicians, female dancers, acrobats, chess-players and cooks.

The high number of human sacrifices revealed by the diggings at Anyang has given Marxist-minded Chinese scholars an argument in favour of a traditional, *a priori* pattern of historical evolution. According to them, such sacrifices furnish the proof that Chinese society in the Shang period was based on slavery. But in view of all we know of this practice in China itself and in other ancient civilizations, it seems hardly credible that the men who were sacrificed with the deceased should usually have been mere slaves. Rather, it would seem that most of the people who accompanied the kings to their tombs were household servants, intimate friends, hunting companions and wives.

THE PERIOD OF THE HEGEMONS

4

THE PERIOD OF THE HEGEMONS

Transition between the Archaic Period and the Period of the Military States [7th and 6th Centuries B.C.*]*

1 Changes in Economy and Manners

We have good reason to postulate a gradual increase in population and land cleared for cultivation in North China between 1000 B.C. and 700 B.C. Admittedly, recent excavations have proved that tools and agricultural implements did not change much between the Shang and Chou periods, but the fact that wild fauna withdrew from the region is fairly reliable proof of a growth in population and a change in the relationship between man and his natural environment.

Certain tropical animals such as the elephant and the rhinoceros either disappeared or became rarer and the eighth and seventh century Chinese do not seem to have brought back as many victims from their hunts as their ancestors did in the Shang period, when the great royal hunts of the fourteenth to eleventh centuries must have been particularly destructive (1). On the other hand, tradition seems to confirm the hypothesis of a progressive clearance of the land during the centuries following the end of the Shang period. The Chou were reputed to have given preference to growing cereals and, according to legend, the

Chinese kingdoms and principalities at the end of the

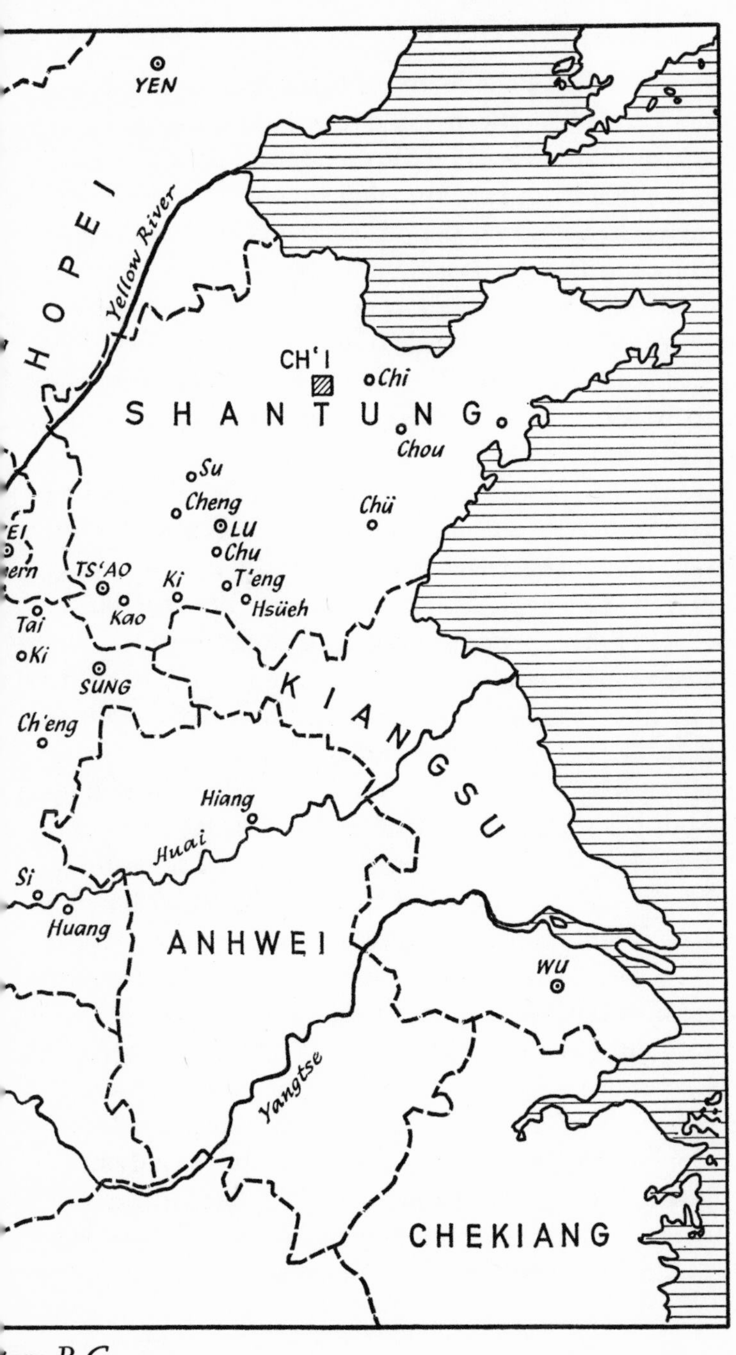
YEN
HOPEI
Yellow River
CH'I
Chi
SHANTUNG
Chou
Su
Cheng
Chü
LU
Chu
TS'AO
Ki
T'eng
Kao
Hsüeh
Tai
Ki
SUNG
KIANGSU
Ch'eng
Hiang
Huai
Si
Huang
ANHWEI
WU
Yangtse
CHEKIANG

ury B.C.

ancestral founder of the house of Chou had been 'minister of agriculture' under the mythical ruler Shun.

Sheep and cattle breeding also seems to have diminished during the first half of the first millennium. When sacrifices were made in the Chou period, ancestors were no longer asked how many animals should be put to death, as in the Shang period. The number was governed by ritual and was reduced to only a few animals (the most common sacrifice had analogies with the Roman *suovetaurilia*). Sacrificing animals by the dozen—so frequent in the Shang period—now seems to be entirely a thing of the past. Writing furnishes additional proof of this reduction in stock-breeding which was to continue until about the beginning of the Christian era: many characters relating to stock-breeding and animal sacrifices disappeared from the vocabulary between the Shang period and the seventh century (**2**).

Archaeological evidence and texts therefore seem to confirm a likely enough hypothesis: the Chinese of the Shang and early Chou periods had heedlessly destroyed natural resources whose wealth must have seemed inexhaustible to them. But this thoughtless destruction of forest and fauna did more than gradually change natural conditions for it transformed the very way of life of the noble class. Limited as it was, it still increased the relative importance of agriculture in the economy, and cereals in the diet. A ritual to regulate hunting (and also tree-felling), established in conformity with the cycle of the seasons, must have seemed necessary from the end of the archaic period onwards. Condemnation of the great hunts, which resulted in an over-rapid destruction of game, and which were held out of the ritual season was to be one of the favourite themes of Confucian morality in the time of the Warring States. But perhaps this theme dates even further back.

The control of hunting may also have played its part in the formation of a new ethic. More generally, we may assume that the position which cereal-growing seems to have acquired at the expense of hunting and stock-breeding had certain indirect effects on Chinese mentality and ideas in the Western Chou period. It would seem that ritual took an even firmer hold during this period—of which we still know little—and that a spirit of moderation had begun to rule the behaviour and relations between noble families. This simple enough theory is borne out by the differences in mentality between the periods; when one compares the luxurious and violent behaviour that was so current in the Shang period with the behaviour of the seventh and sixth century nobles who were so mindful of ritual and preoccupied with moderation it is only reasonable to suppose that there had been an evolution. Recent excavations have also revealed that ritual control—at least with regard to funerary practices—had become far stricter by the end of the Western Chou period and at the beginning of the Ch'un-ch'iu period, whereas it was to become increasingly lax from the late sixth century onwards. It may be equally significant that the number of men sacrificed with the deceased was so much smaller during the first millennium, as we have already noted. By the time of the Chou, the Chinese seem to have forgotten the hecatombs of the Shang period. At least diggings have still to reveal tombs of later date than the Shang period but containing as many human remains. Should we see in this signs of a progessive spirit of moderation, and a general condemnation, not, perhaps, of sacrificial murder, but at least of *hubris*?

Another important factor was that Chinese cities of the seventh and sixth centuries B.C. began to engage upon a form of courtly warfare. This was a carefully regulated kind of tournament, a battle for prestige, in which only moderate use of violence was permitted. Anyone making abusive use of force and profiting from the weakness of the enemy lost his honour and was very likely to bring the wrath of the gods upon himself (3).

2 Formation of the Chinese States

Other less hypothetical changes took place during the same period. They were to have a decisive effect on the evolution of the Chinese world and the course of its history. Between the end of the Shang period and the seventh century, the palace-city civilization had spread throughout the area between the northern steppes and the Yangtse basin. We know for certain that even at the beginning of the Chou period there was at least one Chinese settlement in a region as remote as the lower Yangtse—more than 600 miles from the original cradle of Chinese civilization. This is proved by the inscription on a bronze vase discovered east of modern Nanking (4) in 1954. New centres were established wherever natural conditions were favourable (sources of water, communication routes by water and land, fertile land, pastures) and there privileged sites must certainly have been inhabited as early as the Neolithic periods.

Some of the new cities were powerful enough to impose their authority on neighbouring towns and chiefdoms by means of force or diplomacy; they managed to surround themselves with vast territories and, by the seventh and sixth centuries already had the aspect of capital cities. Consequently, the term that was first used to designate a palace-city, isolated in the midst of its forests and marshes, now came to be used for kingdoms consisting of a group of towns and villages.

Great kingdoms of the seventh and sixth centuries include Ch'i, which dates from the Shang period and whose capital was established in a valley on the northern slopes of Shangtung; Chin, in the Fen basin in Shansi in a region that had been inhabited since Palaeolithic times; and Ch'u, along the middle Yangtse. We could add the Ch'in kingdom in the Wei valley in Shensi. But because of its weakness during this period it hardly compared with the powerful kingdoms of Ch'i, Chin and Ch'u.

The distance between these rich cities and the religious capital of the Chou, their early awareness of their authority and strength, the originality of the local cultures resulting from the contact and eventual fusion of Chinese and natives must all have strengthened the feeling of autonomy and whetted the desire for independence of these outlying Chinese regions. The Chin nobility intermarried with the Barbarians after exchanging womenfolk with the Ti, a non-Chinese people in Shansi. Similarly, the slowly assimilated local Barbarian chiefdoms seem to have played an important role in the formation of the Ch'in nation; its methods of war and the peculiarities of its social organization may perhaps be explained by these native influences. As for the remote Ch'u kingdom, its arts, language and customs made it almost a foreign country in the eyes of the Chinese of the great plain. The discoveries made a few years ago at Changsha in Hunan have confirmed the originality of the artistic traditions of these middle Yangtse peoples (5). The powerful Wu and Yueh kingdoms in the plains of the lower Yangtse and on the shores of the Chekiang estuary appear to have been even further removed from civilization. They were to play an important role in the wars of the sixth and fifth centuries. The Chinese cities founded in these remote regions remained isolated, and acquired a distinctive character of their own after the Chinese had taught the native fishermen and boatmen the art of bronze-casting. As a result, these kingdoms of the south-east developed independently for a time, and were eventually regarded as an alien civilization by the Chinese of the great plain.

It is now possible to explain the cause of the disorders into which the Chinese world was plunged from the beginning of the Ch'un-ch'iu period (722–481). Firstly, it lay in the disparity between powerful cities and weak cities, large and small kingdoms, and, to put it more generally, in the opposition between North and South China. From the seventh to the fifth centuries, the old-established countries of Yellow River China, and in particular the small principalities of Honan, were obliged to defend themselves constantly against the greed of the southern kingdoms and even more against the northward encroachments of the great Ch'u nation.

But even worse was to come. The entire moral cohesion of the Chinese world was threatened from the seventh century onwards when the little cities of the great plain (the term 'middle kingdoms', *chung-kuo*, is still used today to designate China) found themselves faced by the outlying kingdoms who lacked their respect for ritual and moderation. The Ch'u nation had a particularly keen lust for conquest and domination by force, which was completely foreign to the mentality of the ancient Chinese cities. Since it ignored the rules of courtly warfare and was not subject to the same religious scruples it did not hesitate to wipe out its enemies and destroy their forms of worship.

3 The Establishment of Hegemonies

(*i*) *The decline of the Chou*

A more precise reason can be found for the dissolution of the order which seems to have been established among the little cities of the great plain—an unstable order consisting of a balance of power and founded on respect for the noble hierarchy and ritual prerogative. It lies in a political event which resulted in the weakening of the royal house of Chou. Towards the middle of the eighth century, advancing Barbarian populations had forced the Chou to abandon their capital in Shensi and to take refuge in Honan, on the site of modern Loyang. From this moment onwards, the Chinese began to regard warlike power and religious power as independent of each other, although the two had been regarded as inseparable in the archaic period. At first, richer and more powerful cities than that of the Chou gave their protection to the eminent religious centre, the capital. But, since they had no effective power, the kings gradually lost their religious and moral authority in the wars that broke out between Chinese cities. This in turn affected the evolution of Chinese thought. At the very moment when danger was threatening and when, on the other hand, a spirit of conquest and acquisitiveness was asserting itself, the notion of ritual became more explicit and an oecumenical conception of royalty began to take shape.

The seventh and sixth centuries correspond to the period traditionally known as that of the Hegemons. While, in the Chinese world, the religious pre-eminence remained in theory with the house of Chou, powerful kingdoms took over its military pre-eminence and imposed an order that the kings were incapable of enforcing. But the authority of the

Hegemons did not only express itself in military matters, for it was the Hegemon who presided over the rites of alliance between cities.

(*ii*) *The oath of solidarity*

The oath of alliance (*meng*) was a particularly dangerous act because it brought the participants into direct contact with the most formidable of the religious powers. The person of the prince, the city chief or the great officer appointed as delegate for the oath was inviolable. They were already under the protection of the divine powers who were invoked during the ritual (sun, moon, mountain gods and sacred rivers). The oath seemed to create, as it were, family ties between the participants. They were even bound to take part in the funeral ceremonies of those with whom the oath had been taken. The ritual itself called upon the religious powers by an invocation spoken on a mound on which an ox (more rarely, a pig and a cock) had been sacrificed, and also by writing, for the text of the oath was buried with the victim or the remainder of the victim's blood. The invocation was made collectively by 'those in charge of the oath' and was repeated in turn *viva voce* by everyone present, after they had moistened their lips with the blood of the victim.

The purpose of the oath was to renew solidarity between the cities and to consecrate the order established between the chiefs of the principalities. But in the course of the seventh and sixth centuries it tended to become one of the means by which more powerful cities were able to dominate their weaker brethren before resorting to annexation pure and simple—long considered a major act of impiety. As mentioned before, the behaviour of the Ch'u already differed from that of the Ch'i or the Chin. The Ch'u made more frequent annexations and fewer alliances. But in the sixth century, it was inconceivable that annexation itself could be carried out without a solemn triumph and sacrifices, for it implied a wager with destiny and the religious powers. When the Ch'u destroyed the little city of Ch'ai in Honan in 513 B.C., they believed it necessary to sacrifice the crown prince to the mountains. The idea of conquest as a purely positive action of a political and economic nature only arose slowly out of the wars of the next period, between the fifth and third centuries B.C.

4 History

In the political history of pre-imperial China, the period of the Hegemons marks the beginning of a long series of wars and coalitions that were only to come to an end with the unification of the Chinese nation by the Ch'in kingdom and the advent of the Empire. Tradition mentions five Hegemons but only the Ch'i, Chin and Ch'u wielded effective power. The Ch'i first assumed the role of leader of the confederation of eastern cities and guardian of traditions by an oath of alliance made in 667, and did in fact manage to protect the principalities of the great plain against the attacks of the Ch'u kingdom. They were succeeded in their role of protectors of old China by the Chin, who confirmed their position as Hegemon by defeating the Ch'u in 632. But the Ch'u finally won in 597 and their power only diminished in the late sixth century when a new rival appeared—the kingdom of Wu which occupied the south of the modern province of Kiangsu. In 506 the Wu even succeeded in seizing the capital of the Ch'u state, but by the beginning of the fifth century they were menaced in turn by their southern neighbour, the Yueh. In 473, the Wu were destroyed by the Yueh, who then expanded at the expense of the Ch'u. Consequently, the serious threat that the Ch'u had constituted for the cities and small kingdoms of the great plain in the seventh and sixth centuries had lessened by about 500 B.C. But other factors may have contributed to the decline of the Ch'u, including the power of the great noble families who obstructed attempts at political centralization.

The result was that in the seventh and sixth centuries coalitions were set up by the three great kingdoms of the Ch'i, Chin and Ch'u. The little cities of the great plain trapped between these kingdoms of the north and south were subjected to continual threats and pressure and were gradually annexed during the following period.

5 Social and Intellectual Changes

But the cities did not remain idle until they were swallowed up by their more powerful neighbours. They succeeded in uniting to secure temporary peace among the great kingdoms. Being weak, their only resources lay in diplomacy and persuasion. Consequently, during the conflicts that divided the peoples of the Yangtse valley and the Yellow River from the seventh century onwards, they developed a subtle art of diplomatic coalitions and moralizing rhetoric that was to have a very great influence on Chinese thought and literature before the Christian era. When menaced by the outlying kingdoms, the ancient cities held all the more tightly to their traditions, especially as the newcomers were not insensible to what they regarded as authentic nobility and *Chineseness*. The great influence that moral and ritual considerations must then have had on the behaviour of individuals and cities must partly explain the formation at the beginning of the fifth century of that ideal of the honest man which was one of Confucius' main preoccupations.

By contrast, armed conflicts gradually made the Chinese aware of the reality of military and economic factors. Eventually the fortunes of war were no longer regarded as the verdicts of divine judgement but as the logical consequence of the degree of weakness or strength of each adversary. This new, more positive spirit was to lead to a slow decline of the old order. The hierarchy of the nobles and the respect for tradition gave way to relationships based on power, not only between kingdoms but even more within each kingdom. Consequently, from about 600 B.C. a series of violent struggles for power broke out between the great families, besides bitter rivalries between princes and barons, and a dramatic attempt was made by the chiefs of the kingdom to free themselves from the domination of the most powerful families. These struggles sometimes resulted in the elimination of the hereditary nobility in favour of new men who were completely devoted to the prince (as happened in the Chin kingdom at the end of the seventh century) and sometimes in a *de facto* usurpation (as at Lu in 562, where the legitimate prince kept his functions as religious head but lost all real power); sometimes in the complete usurpation of princely prerogatives (at Ch'i in the early fifth century), and sometimes even in territorial divisions (Chin, 453).

Once the fragile barriers imposed by custom had given way all the traditional political and social structures gradually disintegrated. The destructive effect of the desire for power and wealth and *self-interest* (*li*) was stressed by certain leading thinkers in the period of the Warring States and, in particular, by Mencius at the end of the fourth century, in the famous first page of his collection of sayings.

Voluntary, personal, man-to-man relationships took the place of the archaic type of relationship which had been founded on blood bonds and respect for ritual and religious authority. Each great family tried to build up its own client-system. The chiefs of the kingdom were deprived of the effective sources of their power because they no longer received tribute in the form of armed men, chariots and agricultural produce and became personally obliged to collect the soldiers and materials necessary for the maintenance of their power. Professional armies and personal militia were among the novelties of the period.

The sixth century was also the time of the first fiscal and agrarian reforms such as those reported at Lu, a small city-state in Shantung, in 594 and 590, and at Cheng in Honan in 543 and 538 B.C. Whereas in the archaic period the peasantry seems to have been obliged to work for nothing on lands whose produce was reserved for the nobility, the system of grain taxing spread from the sixth century onwards. It was generally a tenth of the yield and seems to have been calculated either according to the annual average or according to the actual production of each year. The practice of taxation in kind was almost certainly accompanied by a noticeable change in the living conditions of the peasantry and no doubt farmers won more liberty and independence in their relations with their former masters. A certain village autonomy may also have developed as soon as a true fiscal system had replaced traditional systems of payment.

The first penal laws, written on iron cauldrons, appear towards the same time in the second half of the sixth century. They are an important innovation for they imply the birth of centralized power and the substitution of written law for the tacit rules of custom which formerly regulated relations between noblemen and country-folk. As political power developed Chinese society tended to become more cohesive. Whereas archaic society seems to have been a juxtaposition of numerous little social groups who were subjected to a large variety of statutes, vaster and more organic societies were now in the process of formation. The division of Chinese society into noblemen (and later scholars, too), peasants, craftsmen, and merchants must certainly date from the period of the Hegemons and was to become traditional under the Empire.

These bitter struggles placed further burdens on the peasantry and Confucian scholars were justified in seeing a connexion between the decline in the authority of the old statutes and the misery to which the peasants were condemned by a nobility greedy for luxury and power. Excavations have furnished valuable evidence of the taste for luxury and scorn for rites that funerary customs revealed from the end of the sixth century onwards. From then on precious objects used for profane purposes took their place beside the ritual vessels in the tombs.

The contrast between modes of behaviour became more marked as the moral crisis intensified, but out of the struggles, disorder, and confusion which shook the Chinese world from the seventh century onwards a system of moral philosophy and positivist thought (**6**) was to emerge.

THE FORMATION OF THE MILITARY STATES

5

THE FORMATION OF THE MILITARY STATES

[From about 500 to 221 B.C.]

1 The Iron Age

During the three centuries preceding the Empire (fifth–third centuries B.C.) the landscape of China and its natural conditions underwent a rapid and complete transformation. Immense areas of land were cleared, drained, cultivated, and often irrigated. Cultivated land reached as far as the frontiers of kingdoms. The population of China as far as the Yangtse basin grew rapidly in spite of the extremely destructive nature of the wars. At the end of the early Han period, in a country whose economy had hardly developed since the third century, it was to reach the figure of fifty-seven million inhabitants (census of A.D. 2) (1). Towns enlarged their walls, filled up with inhabitants, and then surrounded themselves with a second line of ramparts. The importance of kingdoms was now estimated in terms of area and population, not merely by the number of war-chariots. Contemporaries were aware of the profound differences separating their period from that of the Hegemons and still more remote times when the archaic cities only controlled a very restricted and thinly populated territory. It need hardly be added that principles of government were also different.

Problems of administration, subsistence and the use of land scarcely arose or else were resolved fairly easily.

These three centuries roughly correspond to the period traditionally known as that of the Warring States. It was a period whose beginnings were arbitrarily dated to the time of the division of the Chin kingdom in Shansi into three new kingdoms: the Han in Honan, the Wei in south Shansi, and the Chao in the north of the same province. The event occurred in 453. But in order to stress the novelty of the political institutions of this period and the development of state structures inspired by military regimes we have chosen to use the term military states rather than Warring States. We have made use of a less artificial criterion for establishing the beginning of this period—the first evidences of iron-casting (**2**). The first written mention of this technique dates from the year 513 and very recent archaeological finds have allowed us to date the first specimens of cast-iron objects to the early fifth century. We may therefore date the beginnings of this new and final period of pre-imperial Chinese history to about 500 B.C. It is quite certain that the diffusion of iron-casting in the course of the fifth century made it possible for vast tracts of arable land to be exploited, for without this discovery the extraordinary economic development of the Chinese world during the five centuries preceding the Christian era would have been inconceivable. Thanks to the production of a great quantity of implements for agriculture, land-clearing and great irrigation projects, and the increase in agricultural produce attested by the increase in grain taxes, China attained a demographic density and a degree of wealth that gave it a considerable advance over Europe for nearly two thousand years. Iron-casting made its appearance in China nearly 1,600 years before it became known in Europe (**3**).

But no matter how great the importance of this technique, it did not cause decisive changes but only made them possible.

It is true that certain technical or natural conditions favoured a concentration of goods and means of production in China. Iron-casting, which implied a progress in the system of blasting—only possible at very high temperatures—was carried out in furnaces which were massive enough for heat losses to be reduced. This mass production excluded small scale crafts such as the blacksmith's forge—the only iron-working technique to be practised in the West in antiquity and the Middle Ages. Foundries were state enterprises unless they happened to belong to rich merchant-contractors who worked on behalf of the chiefs of the kingdom.

The same applies to stock-breeding, for from the moment the China of the great plains was cultivated and grazing grounds were reduced horses had to be bred in very large stud-farms situated in the steppe regions (bend of the Ordos, Mongolia, north Shensi and Kansu) unless they were obtained in exchange for textiles in official trade with the nomad populations. We may see here how very different conditions were from those in medieval Europe where stock-breeding was only on a small scale.

Similarly, the great problems of draining and irrigation in China applied to vast areas—apart from small scale irrigation works which had certainly been in use locally from a very early period—and could not be solved by the initiative of villages alone. This is why some theoreticians have believed that irrigation is the source of a particular type of political system in various parts of the world (e.g. Wittfogel's 'Oriental despotism').

But although nature and technical conditions promoted the rise of a certain form of state-control in China and, primarily, the evolution of a small group of large-scale contractors and heads of industry, we must look to historical factors for the main reasons for this development.

In the cities of the archaic period, craftsmen's workshops were dependencies of the palace and the free craftsman was unknown. By keeping the main produce of craftsmen under the direct or indirect control of the political power, the military states were not innovating, they were merely following a very old tradition. And it was yet another tradition that encouraged them to reserve the profits of the exploitation of underground resources and of forests and marshlands for the public treasury. Lastly, although the establishment of a system of regulation of water courses and irrigation, and the control of this system, may have affected the political constitution of the military states and imperial China, the fact remains that, historically, it was the pre-existing state structures and the large, well-trained labour force provided by the armies that made the great irrigation projects possible.

Irrigation is only one aspect of the transformation of the Chinese world from the beginnings of the Iron Age onwards and it may not be the most important. In any case, it does not constitute a sufficient explanation in itself.

2 The Reforms

It was also in the sixth century, in a China which was still very poorly exploited and in which great stretches of forest and marshland remained despite land-clearing, that the first signs of changes to come appeared in certain kingdoms. They were as follows: fiscal reforms, written penal laws, and an early type of centralized administrative organization.

A form of warfare which aimed at the destruction of the enemy and the conquest of land made the Chinese of this period aware of the importance of economic and political factors. The archaic order was quite inconsistent with this type of warfare which required unity of command, use of strategy, trained troops and abundant reserves. As armed conflicts increased in bitterness, an attempt at centralization became more necessary, and so the reform movements that had begun at the end of the sixth century continued throughout the fifth and fourth centuries. These reforms were more or less ahead of their time, more or less radical, for different kingdoms but everywhere they had similar aims: to destroy the power of the great families, to strengthen the central power, and to increase resources in manpower and in cereals. In most kingdoms, administrative areas gradually took the place of former fiefs. They formed a network of administrative districts and prefectures that was gradually extended from the conquered regions where it had first been instituted to the oldest territories. It became customary to appoint functionaries to head these departments; they were paid in grain and chattels and had to give a detailed account of their administration at the end of each year. The same system was in force in Wei at the end of the fifth century, where even the highest central administrators and army officials were affected by the reforms; from this period onwards, ministers and generals were chosen by the prince whereas in the past such high posts had traditionally been reserved for members of the great noble families.

A similar purpose lay behind other measures introduced in the Wei kingdom such as the institution of a coherent system of punishments and rewards to select the best servants of the state and keep them in obedience, the general prohibition to criticize the laws of the kingdom, the decreeing of severe penalties for counterfeiters of official seals, diplomas in two parts for the levying of troops (4), the prohibition of the vendetta, which had been the cause of prolonged internal conflicts under the rule of the noble families, and the regulation of a way of life which sought to prevent the formation of groups of dependents and to reserve the privilege of the greatest luxury for the prince alone. The texts of the time are irritatingly laconic for what little information they do give us only makes us all the more anxious to have full details of the reforms of this period. They varied from state to state. In the Han kingdom in the mid-fourth century a reformer (we do not know if his advice was taken) told a prince of the advantages of having his intentions and political decisions shrouded in the greatest secrecy, and recommended a severe control over officials with strictly defined duties. In the Ch'i kingdom, between 356 and 320, various measures were adopted to encourage agriculture and the clearing of virgin lands. Rewards were also provided for anyone who was able to hand in remonstrances to the prince. The ancient custom of the remonstrance, which had once been a duty of the noble councillors, was thus extended to the whole population. In the Ch'u kingdom in the early fourth century, the extinction of all noble privileges after the third generation was decreed, and aristocratic families were deported to more thinly populated regions. Negligent officials had their salaries reduced or abolished altogether and the resulting savings were used for the instruction of professional soldiers.

It was in the Ch'in kingdom that the most consistent and radical reforms were made in the mid-fourth century. They were applied progressively between 356 and 348 and must certainly have followed some methodical plan. Since the local nobility was too poor and weak to put up much resistance, political and social changes went much deeper than in the other kingdoms. Forty-one prefectures were set up to cover the entire territory. All measures of length and weight were standardized. Ancient titles and aristocratic privileges were abolished and twenty new grades of military nobility, with proportional pensions, were created in favour of those who had distinguished themselves in war. The distribution of these titles was governed by one simple, objective principle: the degree of bravery shown in battle indicated by the number of enemy heads cut off. Agricultural production was encouraged by exempting peasants from forced labour if their production exceeded a certain quantity of grain. Vagabondage was forbidden and moving was controlled by the police. The first police registration cards appeared in this period. Wanderers and idlers were made into state slaves. The Classics (odes, history, ritual) which had served as a basis for school-teaching were burned. This measure was to be enforced throughout the Empire immediately after unification.

But the most far-reaching reforms were those which destroyed the old peasant communities in order to subject them to a new form of organization. The peasants were grouped in units of five and ten families constituting paramilitary formations. These groups were placed under a régime of collective responsibility and compulsory denunciation of all misdemeanours. This transformation of rural communities was accompanied by a revolution in the system of laying out cultivated fields and by the destruction of former enclosures. In the final resort, what the legislators were aiming at was not mere change in particular sectors (e.g. organization of the administration and the army) but a radical reform of society itself and a transformation of its way of life, amounting to a veritable revolution. The process begun in the Ch'in kingdom in the mid-fourth century was interrupted by a change of rule in 338, but it was continued and taken even further by the founder of the Empire—hence its great historical importance. The reforms of the fourth century gave the Ch'in their military supremacy, enabled them to obtain mastery throughout China, and also inspired the policies of the first Chinese emperor.

Penal laws and systems of bounties and rewards were of military origin, as was the type of billeting imposed on the peasant communities. The harsh discipline of the army was applied everywhere and the whole reform system was conceived so as to direct all energies towards the single aim of conquest.

3 Warfare

War clearly appears as the main cause of the political and social transformations of China between the fifth and the third centuries B.C. But, in particular, various changes in techniques of warfare seem to have had far-reaching consequences. Among the most notable were the appearance of infantry in the late sixth century, the invention of the crossbow in the fifth century, and the creation of a cavalry corps at the end of the fourth century.

Certain outlying kingdoms led the way in matters of military organization: the kingdoms of Wu and Yueh in the lake and marshland regions of the lower Yangtse which were impassable by chariots were certainly the first to have infantry; in Shansi, the Chin kingdom, which had been fighting in the mountains against Barbarian peoples who fought on foot, was obliged to create companies of foot-soldiers (5) in 540. Its example was soon followed by the

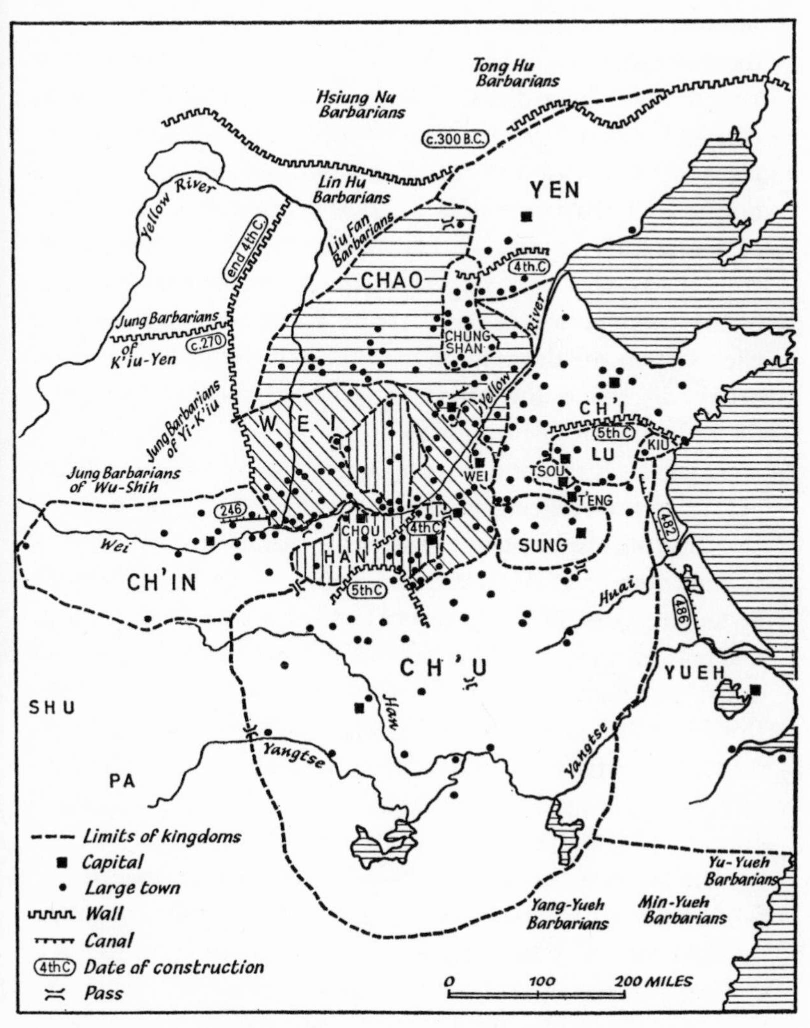

China in c. 350 B.C.

ancient state of Cheng in eastern Honan. The Chin noblemen habitually fought in chariots and did not easily accept the humble role of foot-soldiers that was forced on them. But the way had already been opened for a social transformation which was to have decisive consequences, for once the order and discipline of great armies of foot-soldiers had taken the place of duels of honour and confused mêlées between noblemen's chariots a new world was born. The appearance of the soldier-peasant—a cereal producer and infantryman combined—was certainly the greatest social and political factor in the period of the Warring States. We may judge its effects upon the thought of the time, for the new notions of order, discipline and efficiency were gradually to consign the old concept of honour to oblivion.

The transformation of the armies was gradual. In the period of the Hegemons, they consisted of several hundred chariots followed by some tens of thousands of men, a feebly armed, ragged mob, without training or discipline, which included valets, porters, grooms and sappers. At the end of this period, when conflicts became more intense, the number of chariots reached several thousand for each great kingdom. But from the end of the sixth century onwards, the development of infantry gradually reduced the importance of chariots and their use became restricted. They had not completely disappeared by the third century, but became merely a constituent element in an army largely made up of specialized foot-soldiers such as archers, lancers, crossbowmen and a service corps. The first cross-bow and catapult seem to have appeared in the second half of the fifth century. The cross-bow was wound up with the foot and was far superior to the long-bow in power and range for, according to contemporaries, it could kill the enemy at a range of half a mile.

The intervention of cavalry marked a final stage in the

evolution in methods and techniques of warfare. Once again, it would seem that the pressure and example of border peoples was at the origin of the innovation. In 307, the Chao kingdom, the farthest north of the three kingdoms into which the former Chin state had been divided, formed a cavalry force which was a very close copy of that of its nomad adversaries from the Ordos bend and the Mongolian steppes (**6**). The practice of shooting with a bow and arrow from the back of a galloping horse, which was to be one of the favourite exercises of Chinese horsemen during the Empire, and the trousers which replaced the great robe of the noble classes and which were to be adopted by common people throughout China, both date from this period. It was at the end of the fourth century that warriors on horseback armed with bows—the Hsiung-nu, ancestors of the Huns—came riding out of the Mongolian steppes. The difficult art of breaking in a horse seems to date from about 1000 B.C. among the Indo-Europeans, but does not appear to have been transmitted to eastern Asia until much later. Consequently, there was a marked difference between the civilizations of the West and China: when cavalry was first used in China the essential transformations of society had already taken place. As a result, cavalry was never to be a noble corps; on the contrary, it was recruited from among peasants and often from peoples of barbarian origin. We may therefore say that because of the social evolution of the Chinese world between the fifth and the third centuries and the oblivion into which the aristocratic traditions of the archaic period had fallen, the profession of arms under the Empire was considered to be a lower-class calling.

Cavalry was never very numerous. It was an élite corps with particular functions, and its mobility and speed limited its use to incursions and surprise attacks. On the eve of imperial unification, the most powerful kingdoms only had from five to ten thousand horsemen. Far more than chariots and cavalry, the main body of the army was made up of infantry. Infantrymen came in hundreds of thousands and, considering the very high numbers texts mention, it would seem that almost the whole of the male population old enough to bear arms had been incorporated into the armies as foot-soldiers.

But until compulsory military service had become the rule, recruitment varied according to kingdom and the degree of political centralization. Soldiers were first recruited by means of bounties (in the Ch'i kingdom, eight ounces of gold for each enemy head brought back) or by the promise of exemption from taxes. In the fourth century, the Ch'in kingdom was the first to institute a system of compulsory recruitment for all subjects, thereby setting an example that was to be followed by all the dynasties of the Chinese empire. On the other hand, where aristocratic customs inherited from the time of the Hegemons still survived, the lords formed their own personal militia and this practice was to recur under the Empire whenever the central power weakened. The great army chieftains who played at being proconsul in remote provinces and who resorted to demagogy were also able to transform their troops into private dependents in these periods.

Between the fifth and the third centuries B.C., technical progress, the increased number of combatants, and the necessity for a united command influenced even the forms of warfare. Expeditions went further afield and for longer periods, and the art of strategy developed. Armies were no longer commanded by noble lords or their ministers, all heads of noble families, but by specialists in the art of leading soldiers. In the total war that broke out among the great kingdoms it became more and more obvious that victory in battle depended on the degree of power of each state, i.e. on the number and the morale of its inhabitants, its political organization, agricultural production and grain reserves. Warfare aimed at the destruction of the enemy and the annexation of new territories. It became a war of sieges aiming at the conquest of towns and fortified positions where permanent garrisons were kept. Whereas battles were decided in one or two days in the archaic period, in the fifth to third centuries some sieges lasted more than three years. Towers, ladders on wheels, constructions of heaps of earth that reached the height of the enemies' ramparts, tunnels and mines, bellows to blow smoke in the enemy's tunnels, were all part of the technique of warfare, and fortresses were built in mountain passes or along the frontiers of states. But nobody forgot that the enemy's morale might prove the decisive factor in defeat or victory, and the contestants resorted to propaganda, espionage and ruses (7).

4 The Great Public Works

Everything was in keeping: war required ever increasing resources and better protection against attacks, but the armies provided a very large, well-trained labour force. As a result, states were able to embark on vast schemes of natural development and to build great fortifications. The massive production of cast-iron tools for land-clearing, earth-works and agriculture were of vital importance as they provided the technical means to accomplish such vast undertakings.

The Ch'u and Ch'i kingdoms were the first to build defensive walls along their frontiers during the fifth century, one in Honan, the other in southern Shantung (wall rebuilt or lengthened in 350). Other kingdoms followed their example in the fourth century. In this way, Wei fortified the northern Lo valley in Shensi in 358 and 352, extending the wall as far as the Ordos bend to a distance of over 500 miles. Similarly, Chung Shan, a barbarian principality in north-east Shansi and Hopei, Chao and Yen all built ramparts of smaller size in 369, 356 and 333 to protect themselves in the south. Their effort often confined itself to fortifying the dykes that had already been built along rivers as protection against floods.

In 461, Ch'in had already fortified the dykes of the Yellow River where they faced the frontiers of the Wei kingdom, and then those of the Lo, when the Wei pushed it back westwards as far as the Yellow River valley in 417. In mountain regions, walls took the place of fortified dykes.

Like town ramparts, defensive works built along frontiers were made of pounded earth or, occasionally, of stones. They were reinforced by small forts and defended by troops who were specially selected for the protection of the region. Enemy approach was signalled by smoke in daylight and by fires at night. These measures were a forerunner of the Han Empire's system of defence against the incursions of the Hsiung-nu.

Unlike the walls which served to protect kingdoms against the attacks of their most dangerous neighbours, other fortifications were already intended to protect Chinese territories against the nomad raids from the Mongolian steppes and the Manchurian plain. After campaigns in which the Chinese managed to push the various peoples back towards the north, the far northern kingdoms built great walls in the actual territory of these nomad shepherd peoples. The wall built by the Chao kingdom to the north of the

Ordos bend is of slightly later date than the cavalry corps formed in the same country in 307 B.C. The Yen wall in the Manchu plain must have been built shortly after. In its turn, Ch'in built a wall along its northern frontiers after the destruction of a group of nomad warriors in 270.

From the date of these constructions and the campaigns which preceded them, it would seem that the northern nomads had become far more hostile by the end of the fourth century. But whereas, in about the middle of the sixth century, the Chao kingdom had to defend itself against Barbarian peoples who fought on foot, the Chinese found themselves faced by archers on horseback from the end of the fourth century onwards. These enemies were far more formidable and remained a great source of anxiety to the Han dynasty.

In order to defend itself against the Barbarians of the steppes, the Empire simply continued and perfected the work of the military states, as it did in so many spheres. The great wall of Ch'in Shih Huang-ti, the first Chinese emperor, which protected northern China against the incursions of the Hsiung-nu during the Ch'in and Han dynasties, was created by connecting up the walls that had already been built by the Yen, Chao and Ch'in kingdoms in the late fourth and early third centuries. These walls were extended to the west as far as southern Kansu, and to the east down to the sea, to the Liaotung gulf, and formed a continuous line of defence more than 2000 miles long. It will be noted that these fortifications, remains of which have been found by archaeologists, were built much farther to the north than the fifteenth century Ming walls of which substantial remains can still be seen today.

Warfare called for an increase in agricultural production and explains the number of great works of drainage and irrigation carried out in the period of the Warring States. The first canals had been dug in the beginnning of the fifth century. The Wu kingdom linked the Yangtse to the Huai by a canal in 486 and in 482 it prolonged this waterway as far as the rivers in south Shantung. It cannot be mere coincidence that the Wu was both one of the first kingdoms to form an army of foot-soldiers and one of the first to undertake great irrigation works. Its example was followed by the Wei kingdom at the end of the fifth century, when a canal was dug along the confines of the modern provinces of Honan and Hopei. Other canals were also built in Wei in the course of the fourth century, one being dug in 360 to connect a lake to the Yellow River, the other in 339 in the region of modern Kaifeng. At the end of the third century, the Ch'in kingdom dug a great canal north of the river Wei and running parallel to it; this enterprise was believed to have brought the Ch'in a surplus of wealth that allowed them to complete the conquest of the other Chinese states in a very short time.

But irrigation canals were far from being the only water-works. Depressions in the ground were transformed into reservoirs, dykes were built along rivers and water-ways liable to dangerous floods, locks governed the flow of certain waters and rivers were diverted from their course by dams. The most famous of these great hydraulic works was that carried out on the upper course of the Minkiang, a great tributary of the Yangtse in Szechuan, in about 300 B.C., after the conquest of the Chengtu plain by the Ch'in kingdom. A great dam made it possible to direct the course of the Minkiang into a channel dug through a mountainside. The prosperity of the Chengtu plain dates from this achievement for the plain could now be farmed regularly, without fear of floods.

Although great works of irrigation were still rare in the fifth century, they multiplied during the fourth and third centuries. The same applies to other achievements: the fifth century saw the first appearance of inventions such as metallic coinage, defensive walls, cast-iron implements, etc., while their development and diffusion throughout the Chinese states took place in the fourth and third centuries B.C.

5 Development of Handicrafts and Commerce

At the moment when the central power consolidated itself in every kingdom and an administrative organization was formed, the increasing prosperity of the Chinese world created new social groups, whose activities did not directly encourage either agricultural production or warfare. This phenomenon, running parallel to the consolidation of the state, was a threat that worried the leaders and theoreticians of tyranny. We find certain authors of that time making the distinction, which was still to inspire statesmen under the Empire, between essential activities (*pen*), i.e. the production of goods indispensable to life (cereals and textiles), and secondary or superfluous activities (*mo*), i.e. craftsmanship, free trade and, in a very general fashion, all artistic and intellectual activities.

We have many proofs of the appearance of these new social groups, the first, though indirect, proof being furnished by the rapid development of urban settlements between the fifth and third centuries B.C. The palace-city of archaic times and the period of the Hegemons was a military, political and religious centre which only housed the nobles and the personnel and craftsmen employed by the palace. The ramparts were generally no more than 400 to 600 yards in perimeter. By contrast, the fourth and third century towns whose sites have recently been excavated were surrounded by walls as much as two miles long, and texts which confirm these dimensions enable us to estimate the population of the greatest Chinese cities of this period at several tens of thousands of inhabitants. They were often protected by a second line of ramparts which provided shelter for the country-folk in time of war. The largest city of the fourth to third centuries was probably the capital of the Ch'i kingdom in Shantung, a city made prosperous by its trade in bronze, textiles, salt and fish. Certain texts give it a population of 70,000 families, i.e. more than 300,000 inhabitants, but this may be an exaggeration. In any case, it is in this town that we find the strongest evidence of the presence of an urban class of free craftsmen, small merchants and artists. Each trade had its separate district. Games and amusements had an important place in the lives of the citizens, and the town was famous for having an academy where moralists and political theoreticians held debates.

To conclude, at the time that states were becoming rich by exploiting forests and marshlands, and from great state enterprises such as mines, foundries, pottery workshops and salt factories, a new class of craftsmen and small private shopkeepers arose, with the sole purpose of satisfying the need for luxury of an urban class in full expansion. The period of the Warring States was distinguished by technical progress in most of the crafts, as in the case of metallurgy (bronze alloys, soldering and inlaying), weaving, woodwork, lacquer and ceramics. Even so, the states tended to gain from this progress for they made large profits out of the great many taxes they imposed on free trade (compound duties, taxes on shops, market sites and produce). This fiscal system and the development of free trade explain the diffusion of currency at the time of the Warring States.

The first metallic coins, cast in bronze, date from about 500 B.C. according to Chinese archaeologists. They were fairly heavy pieces shaped like spades or knives. It may be that these metal objects first served as means of exchange in the country. At the end of the fourth century, Mencius mentions the custom of bartering metal implements for grain and we should note that, according to the monetary conceptions of the Chinese, metallic currency was associated with cereals and textiles. For a long time, the essential monetary problem under the Empire was to balance the production of cereals against the volume of money in circulation. Although coinage appeared in the fifth century, it did not become currently used until the fourth century, when coins were less heavy and cumbersome and had acquired a nominal value. They were stamped with the name of the place where they had been cast (capital of a kingdom or an important town) and with their value. Recent discoveries have established a list of ninety-six different places of casting. Four types of coinage were current in China in the fourth and third centuries. The areas in which they were diffused were relatively well-defined and correspond to four zones which differ sufficiently for them to be considered as types of cultural area. They were as follows: the Shansi region and its confines in Honan and Hopei (the countries of the 'three Chin'; Han, Wei and Chao) where spade-shaped coins were in circulation; the kingdoms of the north-east (Yen in Hopei and Ch'i in Shantung) where coins were knife-shaped; the Wei valley in Shensi (country of the Ch'in) where round coins with a central circular hole were used; lastly, the sphere of influence of the Ch'u kingdom (middle Yangtse and Han valley), where use was made of gold coins shaped as tablets divided into sixteen little squares carrying the indication of their value, and where bronze cowrie shells were also struck, in imitation of the little shells which were fertility symbols with magic powers—as well as being ornaments, greatly prized for their value in the archaic period.

The institution of written contracts appears to date from the same period, and also led to the development of commerce. The principle of contracts, bearing different names, was the same as the principle guiding the use of the instruments for the transmission of orders in state administration. Each party to the contract kept one half of a wooden tablet or a bamboo stick broken in the middle, and if the two could be joined again this was sufficient proof of the authenticity of the document.

In the fourth and third centuries, conditions were favourable for the development of a commercial mentality compounded of calculation, foresight and cunning. The many close ties between the rulers of the kingdom and the great merchants to whom they accorded the right to exploit large-scale enterprises such as mines, salt-works and foundries, enabled them to profit from the merchants' advice and to share their outlook. The influence of the mentality of this little group of rich merchants is apparent in the political theories aiming at strengthening the central power. Whereas the régime of the high nobility and the tyranny of custom and ritual had put countless obstacles in the way of this small social group, political centralization, the uniformity of the laws and social levelling created conditions that were particularly favourable to its development.

6 History

The military history of the period of the Warring States is an extension of that of the sixth century. We find the same confused list of battles, alliances and temporary coalitions. Tradition tells of seven powerful kingdoms who entered the lists in this period: the 'three Chin' (Han, Wei and Chao) in Shansi, Ch'i in Shantung, Ch'in in Shensi, Ch'u in Hupei and Yen in Hopei. But Yen, whose capital was situated near modern Peking, and Chao—the two most northern kingdoms—played a relatively minor role. In the final analysis, they were hardly more important than Yueh, whom tradition may have excluded from the list of great kingdoms because it was semi-barbarian. Yueh occupied the whole region of the lower Yangtse after it had annexed the Wu nation in 473, but it was wiped out in its turn by the Ch'u kingdom in 306.

From the fifth to the third century, the ancient principalities of Honan and the regions bordering this province were gradually eliminated. For a time, they played a part in the see-saw politics of the great powers trying to set them against one another and encouraging truces, but they were gradually swallowed up by the great kingdoms surrounding them (Han, Wei, Ch'in, Ch'i and Ch'u). Of these five adversaries, united by self-interest or a common danger depending on the fortunes of war and diplomacy, it was the kingdom of Wei that seemed to be most active and powerful in the fifth century. Its position in the Fen valley and the political reforms it applied so soon explain its relative and temporary supremacy. But from the middle of the fourth century, a little kingdom which had hitherto been almost isolated and backward began to constitute an increasing threat to the other Chinese states. Sheltered by the passes that separated the Wei valley from the plains of Honan, the Ch'in kingdom soon became an unassailable citadel which seems to have derived a sudden energy from the great reforms of the mid-fourth century. In 328, it captured the north of the modern province of Shensi, and pushed the nomads of the steppes far back from the vital centre of the Wei valley. In 316, its armies advanced into the Chengtu plain and in 312 occupied the whole of southern Shensi, thus gaining control of the upper course of the Han and menacing the old Ch'u kingdom. Even more decisive was the access to Honan which became possible when Ch'in occupied the western part of this province in 308. While continuing to fight against Wei and Han, Ch'in attacked the west and the south. The need to form a common front against this advance of the Ch'in kingdom led to more or less firm alliances between the states of the north and south, which the Ch'i sometimes joined. But Ch'in's threat to the independence of the other Chinese states became most evident at the end of the third century, for between 230 and 221 it conquered the whole of China from the Mongolian steppes and the Manchu plain to the mountain regions south of the Yangtse in a series of lightning campaigns of an almost Napoleonic brilliance.

THE PROGRESS OF IDEAS DURING THE FORMATION OF THE MILITARY STATES

6

THE PROGRESS OF IDEAS DURING THE FORMATION OF THE MILITARY STATES

The transformations of Chinese society resulted in an extraordinary intellectual ferment from the beginning of the fifth century onwards. Schools of thought and political theories must be considered in order to understand history for, in their way, they mirror the conflicts of the period and by stimulating a spirit of reflection, thorough investigation, and awareness, they act in turn on the process of historical development. It is not an exaggeration to say that we find in the Ch'in Empire the conscious and systematic realization of a theory of the state as first defined in the period of the Warring States. The moral conformism instituted under the Han was merely a revival of the traditions left by certain leaders of schools of thought during the centuries preceding imperial unification, but in a new context, namely that of an Empire built along the lines of a single state.

The progress of ideas confirms the evolution that history has been obliged to recognize. Each period has problems of its own and, inversely, it would be a great pity to dismiss the precious data of history when judging the significance of theories and controversies. If we have only a confused, abstract picture of the three centuries which saw the collapse of the archaic structures, the development of a system of clients, the birth and development of the state, the advent of the soldier-peasant, the appearance of the merchant-contractor and the salaried official, we shall be condemning ourselves to the same confusion between forms of thought which only make sense within their historical context.

The first schools of Chinese thought must again be considered in the context of a society based on the client-system. The client-system arose out of the decomposition of archaic society in the sixth century and was fostered in every kingdom by the increasing wealth of the Chinese world between the fifth century and the foundation of the Empire. The powerful nobles, great ministers and leaders of kingdoms maintained a court of men-at-arms, entertainers, buffoons, musicians and fencing experts, apart from their personal militia—people, in a word, who were skilful in various arts and techniques, and who included wranglers, diplomats and sages. They occasionally acted as councillors and would address remonstrances to their masters. If these masters of morality and politics were famous, then, they in turn would have their own clique, mostly formed of several dozen disciples who followed them everywhere. These disciples would sometimes number several hundred, and the more or less organized school they composed would then be a kind of sect. The chiefs of the schools and sects would go from kingdom to kingdom offering their services to the princely courts or the houses of the great nobles and would have themselves maintained by all those who wished for men of exceptional wisdom. The custom sometimes gave rise to institutions such as the academy founded at Lin-tzu, the capital of the Ch'i kingdom, in the second half of the fourth century, where masters of different schools of thought were maintained at the expense of the prince. Certain borrowings and mutual influences among the schools may have arisen from the palavers of the Lin-tzu academy.

1 Fifth Century Thinkers: Confucius and Mo-tzu

The earliest leader of a school of thought was Confucius (K'ung-tzu). He was a noble, although not a member of the high nobility, who still bore the stamp of the moral attitudes that had once been the sole preserve of the noble class, such as moderation, respect for rites and loyalty to the ancient traditions so jealously preserved by the old principalities of the great plain. He seemed to belong to the fringes of high society, to the very ancient and no doubt highly conservative little group of assistants to the noble power, such as scribes and specialists in divination. There is evidence to support this. The venerable writings that were handed down amongst this group (harangues of the old kings, religious hymns and court poems, divination manuals and annals of the kingdom) played a larger part in Confucius' education than warlike instruction. Archery was no more than a ritual ceremony for him and there lay its only interest. He was not in the least interested in driving chariots and, as he was not involved in the duels of honour and fights for power which were the sole occupation of the great families of his period, he was able to appoint himself the judge of their behaviour in the name of the tradition he represented. The neglect of rites among the nobility, their taste for luxury and the development of a new mentality in contrast to the old spirit of moderation led him to define the ideal of the honest man: a man whose training was more bookish than warlike —already almost a 'man of letters'—who was concerned with correct behaviour and ritual gestures and attitudes. His moral system forbade compromise (especially in the delicate question of relations between the Wise Man and the authorities) and yet it was entirely flexible and not at all harsh. It rejected all *a priori* judgements and all abstract principles, arising as it did from reflection on matters of conduct and a subtle analysis of the slightest nuances of behaviour. Adroitness, psychological penetration, and a just appreciation of circumstances were what was required by a morality that was both born out of ritual and founded upon it. This is what gives Confucius' teaching its charm and human warmth. The beautiful ideal of constant reflection and unceasing efforts at self-improvement was inspired by the spectacle of the decadence of ancient customs. To remain faithful to traditions—was this not necessarily to transfigure them?

The school of Confucius may perhaps have arisen from the academies where young noblemen were formerly trained. If Confucius proposed to revive the society of his time by ritual and by morality it was because this society still had only an embryonic administrative organization, and it seemed that order could still be ensured by a respect for the hierarchies and customary statutes.

Later, by contrast, there appeared a leader of a school who apparently stood for the very low nobility that formed the majority of fighting men (*shih*) in armed expeditions, and who was to denounce the fundamental vices of this society. For Mo-tzu (late fifth century and very early fourth century), the clan spirit and competitions for prestige were the root of all the ills of his time, such as wars between cities, fights between great families, sumptuary expenses and the misery of the common people. He was also a moralist but one inspired by an egalitarian ideal. He wanted to replace family egotism and the customs that were inseparable from the system of clients by a generalized altruism. Instead of sumptuary practices and the monopolization of wealth and women by the great families he proposed a uniform control of expenses and ways of life (but not that hierarchized control which was to remain the ideal of the Confucian school), and his general condemnation of homicide doubtless implied the institution of public justice and the prohibition of private vendettas. Mo-tzu was the partisan of an autocratic power based on the poverty-stricken class that was so close to the peasantry and that was his own. We may understand, then, why it was that from the end of the fifth century to the foundation of the Empire Mo-tzu's ideas had much greater influence than the aristocratic ideal of the honest man that Confucius had proposed. Mo-tzu's school also rather resembled a sect. It was organized, it had its rules and its leaders and it practised what it preached. Its members dressed like the peasants or craftsmen of the time and intervened to stop wars or to defend cities that had been unjustly attacked. Techniques of town defence were taught in the school, and several chapters of the work attributed to Mo-tzu deal with this subject in detail.

But the sect also taught the rules of preaching, for one of the main activities of the faithful was to make new converts and to convince the powerful of their injustice and impiety. The disciples and heirs of Mo-tzu were the first to lay down the principles of an art of speaking and it was in their midst that the first dialecticians appeared.

However, other currents were also to assist the development of a Chinese art of sophistry in the fourth and third centuries: on the one hand, the ancient custom of diplomatic palavers, and on the other, the court games. Amongst jugglers, jesters and buffoons, certain verbal games were played such as guessing games, paradoxes and reasonings with absurd conclusions; in all such games the influence of a kind of international folk-lore has sometimes been suspected. These combined traditions seem to have given rise to a current of thought somewhat reminiscent of a fundamental orientation of Greek philosophy, for it was problems of logic and physics that occupied the minds of the Chinese sophists. Unfortunately, the texts which inform us about this emergent philosophy have suffered greatly and allow us only a glimpse of the kind of questions that the sophists and the heirs of Mo-tzu (1) asked themselves. In any case, contemporaries took no interest in their experiments and at a time when the moral crisis was felt so profoundly, and when practical problems of administration and warfare were claiming all their attention, they regarded such attempts at the correction of language and the strengthening of the state as a futile game which could only be harmful to ritual.

2 The Partisans of Individualism and Anarchy

Whether they entirely rejected tyranny, wished for it to last for ever, or sought to soften its rigours, the different schools of thought that arose in the fourth and third centuries must all be defined mainly in relation to the form of state power that had arisen from military and economic necessities.

Certain anti-social and anarchistic tendencies appeared as early as the time of the Warring States and under the Empire they continued to stimulate one of the most original and lively currents of Chinese thought. The Taoist school which included a writer of genius, Chuang-tzu, was at the head of these tendencies, but presumably there existed a wider current which overlapped it. The condemnation of luxury, artifices, techniques and institutions, was common to a whole number of school leaders, all more or less closely related to the Taoists. Sometimes they insisted on one rule for living, sometimes on another: some suggested that one should never reply to an affront, seeing in this the universal means of securing peace among men; others recommended indifference, a spirit of nonchalance and an egotistical reserve; others praised the benefits of individual autarchy and wished each man to provide for himself and his needs. They all recommended an ideal of frugality and autonomy, and must have been thinking of the living example furnished by the smallest and most isolated of the rural communities.

For the Taoists, the dark ages when men knew nothing of the refinements of civilization were a golden age; each technical advance and each new institution represented yet another step towards the final enslavement of man and the degradation of his natural virtues. The same taste for the primordial and the indistinct is found in their attitude to ideas: like the sophists, the Taoists enjoyed trying to solve antimonies. All distinctions were artificial. Large and small, life and death, only had meaning with reference to each other, but, in an absolute sense, they were equivalent. Everything was in everything.

Total rejection of the use of reason, refusal of community life and its constraints, and withdrawal into oneself, were all taken to extremes by the Taoists. But should we not consider this a healthy reaction against the progress of tyranny?

Certain currents of thought deriving from the remote past were not altogether lost despite the development of moral reflection and rational thought between the fifth and third centuries, and it was mainly due to the Taoist milieu.

Whereas the concept of a cosmic order serving as a model for human conduct and the idea of the universal efficacy of rites constituted the basis of moralistic thought, the traditions peculiar to diviners, specialists of the *yin* and the *yang*, and rain-making sorcerers, and a whole heritage of magico-religious beliefs and techniques (among others, exercises in breath-control, mental concentration and sanctifying diets) were also handed down during the three centuries made famous by so many original thinkers. This current of superstition ignored the many, very early empirical discoveries of the Chinese which so astonish the historian of science (**2**). We shall see these traditions coming back in force during the Han period when the great problem of social and political order seemed resolved.

3 The Theoreticians of the State

In the fourth and third centuries, the Taoists and all who resembled them were opposed by the realistic and far-seeing theoreticians of the State.

Since self-interest, the root of disorder, had become the reason for all conduct and since punishment alone could prevent passions from running riot, the new order had to be founded on self-interest and fear and not on a morality that had been proved ineffective everywhere. A judicious system of punishment and reward, based on acquisitiveness, the desire for titles, and the fear of torment should be enough to preserve the State from ruin and, in addition, to safeguard its military supremacy. But everything had to depend directly on the prince, for if he were to delegate the least part of his powers to a third party there would be a revival of the client-system and disorder would reign again. Punishments and rewards, given in public and known to all, were an objective and impartial means of government as were all the methods of proof and instruments for the transmission of orders like official seals, diplomas in two parts, ciphered accounts, written administrative reports, and anything that facilitated effective control of civil and military officials and helped to ensure their strict compliance with the prince's orders. Sincerity, devotion and loyalty were superfluous. The question of selecting the right men, which still seemed so important to Mo-tzu and which continued to preoccupy moralists, was merely a false problem. The old notion of government by the best, which assimilated nobility and individual worth (virtue being revealed by tests and supernatural signs) was rejected. The official of the new State was an interchangeable man of average ability whose conduct was necessarily guided—as was that of all other subjects—by a body of legal rules constructed from the most basic elements of a common psychology (desire for wealth and social elevation, fear of punishments). But why did the *legalists* have such confidence in objective means of proof, and why this deliberate recourse to writing? The fact was that such procedures had already proved valuable not only in the administration of certain kingdoms but also in large-scale commerce and important enterprises (mines, foundries, salt mines, large craftsmen's workshops). A new mentality was born among the small group of rich merchant-contractors who were accustomed to calculations, to the use of money and contracts, who speculated on the desire for gain and for luxury, and who profited from the elementary but efficient psychology they had learned from their experience of commercial dealings. They were in close contact with the rulers of the kingdom, often administrating enterprises on their behalf, and sharing the profits. They had interests in common with the prince since they too benefited from political centralization, uniform legislation and measures, and the disappearance of the client-system and privileges. Some merchants acted as advisers to the princes, like Fan Li, minister to the King of Yueh, who was one of the first, around 500 B.C., to recommend 'the enrichment of the State and the reinforcement of the armies', Pai Kuei, who was both a merchant-contractor and hydrographical engineer and who served prince Hui of Wei as minister, and Lü Pu-wei, a merchant and son of a merchant who was adviser to the prince of Ch'in in the mid-third century.

All these men were distinguished by their positive and rational way of thinking, but its application remained limited since the success of commercial enterprises is not determined by calculation and reflection alone and luck, astuteness and flair play an important part. Similarly, the government of men cannot be an entirely rational affair. It is worth noting that the ideas of luck, cunning and secrecy sometimes occupy a greater place in the thought of the men known as the legalists than more positive procedures such as the promulgation of the laws, the system of rewards and punishments, and administrative practices. The links between legalist thought and the mentality of the first Chinese businessmen become evident as soon as they have been mentioned.

Law, as conceived by the legalists, did not have the abstract and general character we might be tempted to ascribe to it. It was not a convention that had been established between men so as to ensure order. Nor was it simply a means of repressing misdemeanours. It went much further than that: what the legalists were aiming at when they introduced a system of punishments and rewards was an order which would function automatically and which, in short, would owe nothing to artifice. The purpose of the law was to accustom the subjects to new ways of behaviour, since the traditional pattern of behaviour had become the main cause of disorder and because a reform of manners seemed indispensable. Law was supposed to have an educational function in the long run. For the legalists, as for the moralists who were the heirs of Confucius, the ideal state was one in which it would no longer be necessary to inflict punishments.

4 Morality and Sociology

We have already said that the problems of logic and physics that so preoccupied the philosophers of the West were of no interest to the Chinese thinkers of the period of the Warring States. They were regarded as an idle amusement at a time when the Chinese people were anxiously wondering how to bring order and peace back to the world. The schools of thought of this period were mainly concerned with problems of government and man as a social being, and there was no question of disinterested speculation.

The vigour of thought we find among the legalists, in works whose realistic spirit recalls Machiavelli's *Prince*, reappears in a third century moralist, Hsun-tzu, who lived between approximately 300 and 230 B.C. and who, together with the legalist Han Fei-tzu, was the greatest thinker of his time. He too had no illusions about man nor was there any place in his thought for supernatural forces or destiny. Man can only count on himself. But, in return, he is master of his destiny. 'Who spends little and works energetically cannot be made poor by Heaven.' But what was Heaven? It was not the divine power that, according to Mo-tzu and the common people of Hsun-tzu's time, brought disaster or good fortune to mankind according to their deeds; it was nature itself, in its order and regularity, as revealed by the motions of the stars and the unchanging succession of the seasons. According to Hsun-tzu, even the abnormal phenomena that give rise to so many superstitious beliefs should be integrated in the norm, for natural disasters, eclipses and prodigies of every kind had occurred at all times and from time immemorial. If they seemed abnormal it was only because they depended on longer cycles than those which could be observed in the course of a human life.

This decision to dismiss all irrational explanations (luck, destiny, religious forces) and to make human conduct dependent on reason alone, expresses the spirit of the age: in Hsun-tzu's time, the efficacy of a disciplined effort in the armies and in the states had been proved. This no doubt explains why Hsun-tzu was able to perceive the social origin of morality and why he was the first sociologist.

A social order corresponded to the natural order: it was created and maintained by the necessities of a communal life and the division of labour. But human appetites and passions produced troubles, conflicts and crimes. Human nature had therefore to be corrected by education and instincts were to be held in check by institutions. Rites and duties gave society its cohesion and allowed honours to be distributed among men. It was thanks to them that each man had the fortune (*fen*) that he deserved. In the last resort, laws alone were powerless to ensure the reign of peace among mankind. Because the laws remain extraneous to the spirit they can only play a subordinate role. Self-control and habits acquired through education are more effective. Similarly, the natural distribution of tasks and occupations that makes society into an organic whole was also more important than laws.

This prime value accorded to morality and to the imperceptible constraint of environment was certainly one of the most characteristic tendencies of Chinese thought. The Chinese attached little importance to objective conventions and rules. Contracts and good faith, law and morality were antinomic. The basis of everything was the inner disposition. True value begins with sincerity, a quasi-religious attitude whose very principle is religious. Indeed, the gods refuse offerings when the givers' intentions are not pure and, as Mo-tzu had said, 'a virtue which does not have its root in the heart is not enduring'.

Despite the profound differences dividing them, the legalists and the heirs of Confucius united in affirming the necessity for a stable order whose maintenance, if not establishment, should owe nothing to artifice or conventions. After the ephemeral dynasty of the Ch'in, the Chinese Empire was to be the common creation of administrators inspired by the legalists and sociological moralists of the Hsun type.

THE EMPIRE

7

THE EMPIRE

So far, the imperial unification of China has given the general impression of a very rapid series of victorious campaigns which enabled the Ch'in to conquer and annex all the other Chinese states. This conquest was also due to the strategic genius and organizing ability displayed by a kingdom that had still seemed particularly powerless and backward at the beginning of the fourth century. But now that diggings have added to our knowledge of the period of the Warring States, the historical evolution becomes easier to follow and it becomes evident that the formation of the Chinese Empire was merely the logical outcome of a slow maturing process which had lasted for three centuries.

The wars of the fifth century broke out between states with entirely different, highly individual cultures which had formed slowly around the little cities founded in the Shang or Western Chou periods, some distance from the original homeland on the great plain. The *de facto* hostility was strengthened by cultural rivalries for although it may now be clear to us that all these warring states shared a common civilization, such a kinship was far from apparent to the peoples of the time. As a result, however, of the continuous mingling of populations caused by the ceaseless bitter conflicts of the fifth, fourth and third centuries, and of the exchanges of hostages, the capture of prisoners, technical borrowings and voluntary or unconscious imitations, war gradually reduced regional differences and peculiarities and created a true cultural community. Recent archaeological finds have given evidence of the slow formation of this spiritual and technical unity in the Chinese world. By the mid-third century, this unity had already been achieved in the minds and customs of the Chinese if not in the political sphere.

1 The Conquest

The economic power of the Ch'in related back to two historical achievements. First came the conquest of the Red Basin, the fertile Chengtu plain in Szechuan, in 316, and the great irrigation works undertaken there in about 300 B.C., and secondly, and even more important, the construction of a 100-mile long canal which linked the Ching and northern Lo rivers and ran parallel to the Wei valley, thus permitting an increase in the yield of the very extensive areas under cultivation.

The Ch'in also revealed the nature of their economic thinking by a practice which seems to have been fairly widespread in certain kingdoms in the late fourth and third centuries and to which they certainly resorted on a wider scale; they would transfer populations in order to balance cereal production and population density. Several such transfers took place in the Ch'in kingdom between 239 and 235, when 120,000 noble families were moved in order to people the region of the capital (modern Hsienyang), on the left bank of the Wei.

But on the eve of imperial unification, the Ch'in nation owed much of its astonishing power to its administrative and military organization which was far superior to that of other kingdoms. The radical reforms of Kung-sun Yang, Lord of Shang, in the middle of the fourth century, had made a genuine state out of one of the most backward Chinese kingdoms. Finally, the measures taken by the reformer Li Ssu (280?–208) during the reign of the last Ch'in prince, the founder of imperial unity, had consolidated the work of Kung-sun Yang.

The man who was to become the first emperor of China, Shih Huang-ti, or to give him his own title, Huang-ti (1) the August sovereign, assumed power in the Ch'in kingdom at the age of 22 in 238 B.C. During the seventeen years that followed he succeeded in subjecting all the other Chinese states to his power. The measures taken to ensure the Ch'in their military supremacy need only be listed to reveal the almost demoniacal spirit that inspired them: they constituted a vast plan for espionage and corruption in which the expenses necessary for bribing the ministers and generals of rival states were part of an overall estimate. In cases where bribery produced no results Huang-ti resorted to assassination. Once treachery was certain and the most loyal defenders had vanished, the Ch'in armies began their offensive. In this way the Ch'in destroyed the Han in 230, the Chao in 228, the Wei in 225, the Ch'u in 223 and lastly the Ch'i, the only adversary still to be feared, in 221.

2 The Unification of China

As soon as they had conquered all the Chinese nations the Ch'in began the gigantic task of giving political and administrative unity to this vast domain. The measures that were destined to create the Empire were even more radical and harsher than those which had been adopted in the Ch'in kingdom in the fourth century.

The total area of the former kingdoms was divided into thirty-six administrative and military districts. Fiefs were definitively abolished, for 'all the wars and all the unhappiness in the world stems from the fact that there are marquises and princes', as later dynasties were also to learn at their expense. Units of measurement that had been used in the Ch'in kingdom since the reforms of the fourth century were imposed throughout the Empire (**2**). China was to have only one type of currency, namely the copper coin, a single type of writing, a single code of penal and administrative laws, and a single type of wheel-base for all carriages. In 220, the Ch'in began to build a network of great three-lane roads, eight yards wide and bordered with trees, to ensure control even of the remotest regions. At the same time, all the fortifications of earlier times were razed to the ground to prevent obstacles being put in the way of the imperial administration and to undermine rebellions. City walls, defensive works in mountain passes and ramparts built by certain kingdoms to defend themselves against attacks by their neighbours, were all destroyed.

The system of collectively responsible family groups was applied everywhere and was to remain in force until the beginning of the Han empire. The penal code as a whole was made more severe and cruel.

It was not only political order supported by police control that the Ch'in meant to impose on the Chinese world, but moral conformism. The strictest puritanism was to prevail everywhere and the conduct of women was subjected to particularly severe laws. Widows with children were forbidden to remarry. Adulterers caught *in flagrante delicto* could be put to death without their assassins being prosecuted (**3**).

Arts and letters were an object of execration to the Ch'in. The classics used in school instruction and all the books that represented 'private knowledge' and 'discredited the present in favour of the past' were destroyed; and only those were preserved that dealt with medicine, pharmacy, divination by the tortoise and milfoil sticks, agriculture and arboriculture. This was the famous burning of books of 213 B.C., which, in fact, seems to have had less serious effects than orthodox tradition complacently affirmed. Confucian men of letters were banished and exterminated as far as possible. All criticism and all discussion was forbidden. Uniformity of thought was to rule everywhere: 'Let the people's only study be the laws of the Empire and let their only masters be the officials appointed by the Emperor.'

There was no room for craftsmen or free trade in this new world. The great merchant-contractors who saw obstacles to their activities in the maintenance of feudal structures before the unification of the Chinese states, and who profited from the political centralization which they had sometimes inspired, were also the first victims of imperial power. The priority given to agricultural production accompanied a repression of all mercantile activities and the concentration of the greatest commercial revenues in the hands of the State. The rich merchants who owned workshops for iron smelting were deported to south Shansi and Szechuan and, according to texts, some 200,000 families of small and large-scale traders were transferred to the Shu state and the Nanyang region, south of modern Loyang, where they were doubtless forced to work in the fields.

3 The Collapse of the Ch'in Empire

This form of absolutist state, inspired by a passion for order and caring nothing for family aspirations, leisure or the arts, could not endure. It collapsed during the years that followed the death of its founder in 210. Ch'in had always been poor and backward (4) and had long been accustomed to the frugal and laborious life to which its princes had subjected it after the reforms of the mid-fourth century. But the other Chinese peoples were more evolved and were unable to bear such a harsh régime. They had preserved their social and cultural traditions despite the political changes which had taken place. Defeat abruptly plunged them into a régime of servitude and austerity. Moreover, all the great defensive works undertaken by the Empire in the steppe region where the threat from the Hsiung-nu was becoming serious led to an increase in poverty and suffering. These were gigantic undertakings such as the building of great roads and postal stages, the sumptuary expenses of the capital where Shih Huang-ti built an immense palace that was completed in 212, as well as exact copies of all the royal palaces of the kingdoms he had conquered, the construction of the colossal and luxurious tomb destined for himself in the side of a tumulus-shaped mountain, and the campaigns fought to extend the confines of the Empire towards the south and to protect it from the steppes. As a result of the general discontent the Ch'in Empire collapsed into anarchy.

When the Han succeeded the Ch'in in 206 B.C. there was a gradual return to the past, a renewal of the client-system, and a renaissance of the traditions dating from before imperial unification. A new personage also made his appearance in Chinese history: the scholar-civil servant who was to be both a legal administrator and an honest man according to the conceptions of Confucius' spiritual heirs. But the administrative organization and underlying state structure of the Chinese world were to remain for ever as a definite acquisition. Although it had been ephemeral, the Ch'in dynasty had succeeded in forging Chinese unity and in making China one of the great empires of all time. It also gave China its name, for it is generally acknowledged that China was first known by this name in the West through the silks manufactured under the Ch'in Empire.

The evolution of the Chinese world was certainly far from complete by the time of the death of the first emperor and the foundation of the Han Empire. As various imperial dynasties succeeded one another China was to be invaded by foreign cultures from the oases of central Asia. On several occasions it was to be either wholly or partly conquered by nomadic peoples from the steppes of Mongolia and the plains of Manchuria. The spirit of China was to be affected profoundly by Buddhism, between the fourth and ninth centuries A.D. and the development of the regions of the lower Yangtse was to lend it new vitality. But all these changes were to take place within a particular context which had been determined since the beginning of the Empire. This vast agricultural Empire formed a remarkably stable world in spite of wars, invasions and revolts, and was to survive the great perils to which the monopolization of land by the rich and Barbarian invasions exposed it.

NOTES

NOTES

Introduction (13–18)

The number of Chinese words in this book has been reduced to the essential minimum. The most widely used system of transcription has been used.

Chapter One (19–26)

1 A total of 128 Shang period sites had been discovered by 1959.

Chapter Two (27–42)

1 See Georges CONDOMINAS, *Nous avons mangé la forêt*, Paris, 1957.

2 Cf. H. MASPERO, 'Contribution à l'étude de la société chinoise à la fin des Chang et au début des Tcheou', in *Bulletin de l'Ecole française d'Extrême-Orient*, vol. XLVI, 2, pp. 360–2.

3 We have adopted the thesis of CHANG KWANG-CHIH, Chinese Prehistory in Pacific Perspective, in *Harvard Journal of Asiatic Studies*, XXII, December 1959, pp. 100–49.

4 H. MASPERO's theory (*La Chine antique*, p. 39) by which the thirty Shang kings cannot have reigned for more than 450 years because 'an average of fifteen years per reign is higher than that of all the historic Chinese dynasties' does not seem to be convincing. The ten reigns of the Manchu dynasty alone cover a period of 268 years. I do not see, therefore, why the reigns of the thirty Shang sovereigns should not correspond to a period of about six centuries.

5 For relations between Shang China and the other civilizations of Asia see LI CHI, *The Beginnings of Chinese Civilization*, Seattle, 1957.

6 A. Leroi-Gourhan, *Bestiaire du bronze chinois de style Tcheou*, Paris, 1936.

Chapter Three (43–68)

1 M. Granet, *Danses et légendes de la Chine ancienne*, new edition, Presses Universitaires de France, Paris, 1959, vol. I, p. 53.

2 M. Granet, op. cit.

3 It is possible that certain of these peoples might have been the ancestors of ethnic groups that were later known in the history of the Far East, such as, perhaps, the Thai, Tibetans, Turco-Mongols, and Ainu. But, need we add that the problem of *races* does not exist? At all times, minglings of strains were too frequent for us to be able to use this term and, even more important, physiological peculiarities count for so little with regard to cultural realities that they are practically negligible.

4 It was probably only in the Western Chou period that kings and heads of cities began to make gifts of land to their high officials and barons. But even then, all that was really granted was the right to a part of the agricultural produce and we would doubtless be mistaken in speaking of 'landed property' for this period. For the opposite argument see H. Maspero, 'Les régimes fonciers en Chine, des origines aux temps modernes', in *Etudes historiques*, Musée Guimet, Paris, 1950.

5 See M. Granet, *Festivals and Songs of Ancient China*, G. Routledge & Sons, London, 1932.

6 Two sites in the Shang style—if not of the Shang period—have been found, one to the south of lake Tung-t'ing in Hunan, the other to the south of lake Po-yang in Kiangsu.

7 A system of harmonies between the cardinal points and basic colour (green, red, black, white and yellow), tastes, seasons and animals was elaborated by ritualists, almost certainly from the end of the archaic period, but its elements must be of even earlier date. In particular, the representation of the world divided into five orientated sectors (centre, east, south, west, north) must date from the very earliest times.

8 The personnel whose names have been found in the *Yi-li* ritual and in the main commentary in the Annals of the Lu nation, the *Tso Chuan*, closely corresponds to that mentioned in

the bronze inscriptions of the Chou period. It has been studied by H. MASPERO, cf. *La Chine antique*, pp. 59–80, and 'Contribution à l'étude de la société chinoise . . .', in *Bulletin de l'Ecole française d'Extrême-Orient*, XLVI, 2, 1954.

9 For the history of weapons in China see Max LOEHR, *Chinese Bronze Age Weapons*, Ann Arbor, 1956, and CHOU WEI, *Chung-kuo ping-ch'i shih-kao*, Peking, 1957.

10 Recent excavations have discovered remains of chariots dating from all the periods between the Shang and the Warring States, so that we can now follow the evolution of the Chinese chariot. The wheel, with a diameter of 1.30 m. to 1.40 m., had eighteen spokes in the Shang period, twenty-one or twenty-two during the Western Chou, twenty-five in the Ch'un-ch'iu period (seventh–sixth century), and twenty-six in the Warring States period. The distance between the wheels varied between 1.80 and 2.30 m., and the shaft, carrying a yoke of 1.40 m. in width, gradually became shorter: although it was nine feet long in the archaic period, it was no more than six feet long by the time of the Warring States.

11 The donor made such offerings as meats and vessels filled with cereals to the gods with his two hands turned upwards. This ritual gesture very frequently appears in the characters of the Shang and Chou periods. Other graphic signs attest to the practice of making libations. Wine was poured on the ground out of vessels that were especially reserved for this rite.

12 It is very probable that this divinatory technique played a great role in the development of writing in China. We should remember that Chinese writing was pictographic in its origins. Some Shang bronzes are engraved with marks in the form of drawings which must certainly correspond to this writing in its most primitive stage. But it evolved towards ideography fairly rapidly and by the fourteenth to eleventh centuries was already very stylized and abounded with abstract formations (opposing or reversed signs, strokes marking a part of a certain sign, representations of human gestures) and above all in characters formed by a combination of the simplest signs. The characteristics of the Chinese language may perhaps explain the formation and persistence of this very elaborate writing system. Monosyllables

were very rich in phonemes and seem to have constituted autonomous linguistic elements in the archaic period, but they did not permit any breakdown of the sounds of the language so that Chinese writing could not develop along the lines of syllabic notation and, even less, alphabetic notation. In general, ten signs corresponded to a single monosyllable and a single linguistic unit.

13 Tombs of the Western Chou period contain a fairly small number of persons sacrificed with the deceased (usually between two and four) and the practice becomes even more infrequent in the period of the Warring States. Out of the 300 tombs of this period which have recently been excavated, not more than ten contain remains of human victims, numbering between one and four for each burial.

Chapter Four (69–86)

1 It would be well worth while to make a study of all known data for the history of fauna in ancient China from inscriptions, figurative representations, old texts and excavation reports. Unfortunately, such a task has yet to be undertaken.

2 For the probable importance of the raising of sheep in archaic China see J. GERNET, 'Comportements et genres de vie en Chine archaique', *Annales, E.S.C.*, 7th year, no. 1, January–March 1952.

3 An excellent account of this type of warfare may be found in Marcel GRANET's *Chinese Civilization*, Kegan Paul & Co., London, 1930.

4 Cf. Sh. KAIZUKA in *Sekai no rekishi*, vol. III, pp. 46–47.

5 Chinese literature is indebted to the Ch'u nation for one of its most beautiful poetic traditions. It is a collection of lengthy, elegiac poems which are believed to be shamanistic in their original inspiration, known as the *Ch'u Tz'u*.

6 A very good account of the essential facts of the history of the Ch'un-ch'iu period is given by T. MASUBUCHI in *Sekai no rekishi*, vol. III, pp. 49–92.

Chapter Five (87–110)

1 More precisely: 12,366,470 families and 57,671,400 individual inhabitants. See H. BIELENSTEIN, 'The Census of China',

in *Bulletin of the Museum of Far Eastern Antiquities*, no. 19, Stockholm, 1947, p. 135. The highest population densities were found in the valleys of the Fen in Shansi, from the Chinkiang to Szechuan and from the Wei to Shensi (the region of Sian especially, where the capital was established, was very densely populated, as was the Loyang region in Honan). Apart from these regions, north-east Honan and southern Hopei, which had been settled in very ancient times, seemed to have kept their economic importance.

2 For the history of iron-casting in China cf. YANG K'UAN, *The discovery and the development of the iron-casting technique in ancient China* (in Chinese), Shanghai, 1956, and J. NEEDHAM, *The development of Iron and Steel Technology in China*, London, 1958.

Cast-iron was of greatest benefit to agriculture, craftsmanship and mining. The iron pieces were far from homogeneous in their composition and broke easily and it was not until the end of the period of the Warring States that the Chinese were able to produce iron weapons by combining casting and forging processes, in the regions of the Yangtse valley (Ch'u state and former Yueh and Wu states) where metallurgical techniques always seem to have been in advance of those in the northern nations.

3 It was also in the period of the Warring States that the science of agronomy seems to have made decisive progress. The first agricultural treatises date from this period.

The history of the swing-plough and the hand-plough in ancient China is still a subject of controversy. But it is still likely that swing-ploughs pulled by animals first appeared in about 500 B.C. and that the first Chinese hand-ploughs date from the end of the period of the Warring States.

4 These two-part instruments (commercial contracts and insignia for the transmission of orders) were originally pieces of bamboo bearing a text in written characters. When the two pieces were fitted together the authenticity of the document was proved. See R. DES ROTOURS, 'Les insignes en deux parties (*fou*) sous la dynastie des T'ang', *T'oung pao*, vol. XLI, 1–3, 1952, pp. 1–148.

5 Cf. S. COUVREUR, *La Chronique de la principauté de Lou*, vol. III, p. 28.

6 Cf. E. CHAVANNES, *Mémoires historiques de Se-ma Ts'ien*, vol. V, p. 77.

7 According to the *History of the Han*, 182 treatises on military art—mostly composed in the period of the Warring States—were collected at the beginning of the early Han dynasty. Specialists in warfare were divided into four groups that might roughly be called: tacticians, strategists, interpreters of signs and emanations, and technicians. Only one of these treatises attained the status of a classic, commentaries on it being written by more than 150 authors. According to this work the main principles that should inspire a leader in war are as follows: i. To know his own strength and that of the enemy. ii. To keep the initiative and leave the enemy in doubt. iii. To deceive the enemy and take him by surprise. iv. To be unseizable, by combining open combat with surprise attacks. v. To manoeuvre rapidly. vi. To adapt one's strategy to the relative importance of the two opposing armies. vii. To ceaselessly observe the enemy during the engagement in order to adapt one's tactics to the evolution of the battle. For the defence of the steppe frontiers in the Han period see H. MASPERO, *Les documents chinois de la 3e expédition de Sir A. Stein en Asie centrale*, London, 1953, pp. 1–13.

Chapter Six (111–126)

1 For the Chinese sophists and logicians see HU SHIH, *The Development of the Logical Method in ancient China,* Shanghai, 1922; H. MASPERO, 'Notes sur la logique de Mötseu, *T'oung-pao*, Leyden, 1927; M. GRANET, *La pensée chinoise*, Paris, 1934, pp. 432–45; Kou Pao-koh, *Deux sophistes chinois*, Paris, 1953.

2 The reader is advised to consult J. NEEDHAM's splendid study, now in course of publication, *Science and Civilization in China*, vols. 1–4, pt. 2 have appeared.

Chapter Seven (127–135)

1 According to most recent studies, the appellation Shih Huang-ti, 'First August Sovereign', does in fact date from after the reign of the first Chinese emperor.

2 A copy on a bronze plaque of the decree by which Shih Huang-ti standardized all the measures in use throughout the Empire was recently discovered at Hsienyang, the ancient capital of the Ch'in empire.

3 Puritanism, which was so noticeable in the Han period and which is usually attributed to the influence of Confucian scholars, might also be a heritage of the Ch'in empire.

4 As late as 361, Ch'in was still considered by the other Chinese kingdoms as a backward and semi-barbarian nation. In 266 a noble of the Wei kingdom made the following judgement on the Ch'in: 'The Ch'in people have the same customs as the Barbarian Jung and Ti. They have the heart of a tiger and a wolf. They are greedy, perverse, miserly and cunning and ready, when their interests are concerned, to make mock of family ties.'

The winter sacrifice that was customary in the other kingdoms was first performed in the Ch'in kingdom in 326. Another sign of the coarse manners that reigned in Ch'in: it was only in 237 that the court abandoned its traditional music which consisted of 'striking earthenware pots and jars and rubbing bones together while crying "hu! hu!" ' in order to adopt the more refined music of the Cheng and Wei kingdoms. It was also said that King Wu of Ch'in died in 307 as the result of a wager whose religious significance is only too obvious, when he tried to lift up a bronze tripod. This was yet another proof of the coarseness of Ch'in people.

BIBLIOGRAPHY

SHORT BIBLIOGRAPHY

As works in Chinese and Japanese have been omitted the following list is very incomplete. Chinese accounts of the very important archaeological discoveries made since the advent of the Chinese People's Republic are not mentioned. However, this deficiency is largely made up by the recent works of CHENG TE-K'UN: *Aspects de la Chine (Langue, histoire, religions, philosophie, littérature, arts)*, ed. Paul DEMIEVILLE, 3 vols., Paris, 1959.

J. G. ANDERSSON, *Children of the Yellow Earth*, London, 1934; 'Researches into the Prehistory of the Chinese', in *Bulletin of the Museum of Far Eastern Antiquities*, vol. XV, Stockholm, 1943.

D. BODDE, *China's first Unifier*, Leyden, 1938.

CHENG TE-K'UN, *Prehistoric China, Archaeology in China*, vol. I, Cambridge, 1959; *Shang China, Archaeology in China*, vol. II, Cambridge, 1960.

CHANG KWANG-CHIH, 'Chinese Prehistory in Pacific Perspective: some hypotheses and problems', in *Harvard Journal of Asiatic Studies*, vol. XXII, December 1959, pp. 100–149.

H. G. CREEL, *The Birth of China*, London, 1936.

W. EBERHARD, *Lokalkulturen im alten China*, Leyden, 1942.

SHORT BIBLIOGRAPHY

M. GRANET, *Chinese Civilization*, London, 1930; *La pensée chinoise*, Paris, 1930.

LI CHI, *The Beginnings of Chinese Civilization*, Seattle, 1957.

H. MASPERO, *La Chine antique*, new ed., Paris, 1955; 'Contribution à l'étude de la société chinoise à la fin des Chang et au début des Tcheou', in *Bulletin de l'Ecole française d'Extrême-Orient*, XLVI, 2, Saigon, 1954.

P. TEILHARD DE CHARDIN and PEI WEN-CHUNG, *Le néolithique en Chine*, Peking, 1944.

A. WALEY, *Three Ways of Thought in Ancient China*, London, 1939.

W. WATSON, *China before the Han Dynasty*, London, 1961.

OTHER BOOKS BY THE AUTHOR

Les Aspects économiques du Bouddhisme dans la Société chinoise du Ve au Xe siècle, Saigon, 1956.

La Vie quotidienne en Chine à la Veille de l'Invasion mongole, Paris, 1959. (*Daily Life in China on the Eve of the Mongol Invasion, 1250–1276*, trans. H. M. Wright, London, 1962.)

INDEX

INDEX

INDEX

INDEX

INDEX

INDEX